Adaptations, 4th edition
© 2022, Anna Frazier

All rights reserved. This book or any portion thereof may not be reproduced or used in any manner whatsoever without the author's express written permission, except for the use of quotations in a book review.

Names have been changed to protect the identities of those who have been written of in this publication. Any resemblance to real people or situations is purely coincidental.

Poems
Published 2022
Edited with Carlos Fernandes II

ADAPTATIONS

Also by Anna Frazier

Elizabeth Young: The Mind's Mess (2020)
The Moon Reaches For Me (2020)
Thank You For The Flowers (2021)
Violet Afternoon (2021)

View other collections at annafrazierpoetry.com.

ADAPTATIONS

poems

by Anna Frazier

Connect

Visit annafrazierpoetry.com to subscribe to email updates on her new collections, view featured poems, and learn more about the author.

NOTE FROM THE AUTHOR
These books are meant to be read in order as well as from left to right. Welcome to a new space.

*In each line's strange syllable: she awakes
as a gull, torn
between heaven and earth.*

*I accept her, stand with her face to face.
— in this dream: she wears her dress
like a sail, runs behind me, stopping*

*when I stop. She laughs
as a child speaking to herself:
"soul = pain + everything else."*

*I bend clumsily at the knees
and I quarrel no more,
all I want is a human window*

in a house whose roof is my life.

— Dedication,
"Marina Tsvetaeva"
Ilya Kaminsky

Being alone boils down to
Turning other people's dark depictions
Into fairytales for my own hope's sake.

— Introduction,
Anna Frazier

CONTENTS

I. Life of the Party

Before Television	2
The Dog	3
Highschool & Then	4
Girls	7
Some Men	8
Let Her Live	9
Breakfast	10
The Agreement	12
The Other Side of Brokenness	13
Saturday Morning	14
A Little Dark Evening	17
If I'll Smile for Anyone	18
Capture	19
Thin Cotton	20
Heart of Many Colors II	23
Find Him	24
A Dark House	25
To Someone Who Isn't	26
The Bad Boy	27
How a Girl Dies	28

Lover's Quarrel	31
PTSD on September 2nd	32
Tell, Tell	33
Court	34
Worn From War	35
A Good Story	36
Black Winter	37
Lines for Turning Aspens	38
Death of a Once-Loved One	41
After I've Died	42
Passerby	43
Funeral for a Twenty-Something	44
Night-River	45
How to Seize the Day	46
The Jacket	49
Bear Crossing	52
Boulder, Colorado	53
The Grind	54
What Capitalism Demands	55
Simple Pleasures From 1935 to Now	57

II. Behind My Eyes

Things We Don't Make Time to Imagine	60

Before Punctuation	63
Autumn	64
A November Week	65
A Sunday Afternoon on the Island of La Grand Jatte, Georges Seurat, 1884	66
Man With No Bags	69
When the Man Falls into a Trap	70
How Could You Not Want to Save Him	71
Talking Parker Down From the Bar Counter	72
November 7th After Riding the Wind All the Way Home	75
The Heart	76
Connection	77
Trapping a Magic Feeling	78
Afternoon Nap to Kill Time	79
When He Left	81
Her Second Sigh	82
In My Story, He Stays	85
Long Lake	86
Nonna Sews a New Wall-Hanging	88
Sun Salutation	89
What Matters	90

HIDING UNTIL LOVE ASKS THAT SHE
COMES OUT TO PLAY   93
CREATION STORY   94
ASKING THE MOON ABOUT MY HUSBAND   95
WHO HAS MY HUSBAND   96
TO THE HUSBAND I HAVEN'T FOUND   99
HOW TO LOVE ME   100
BEFORE PUNCTUATION   104
WINTER MUST MAKE A GOOD WIFE   106
SLATS   109
TO MY SISTER   111
LITTLE GENEVIEVE UNDERSTANDS EVIL   112

III. THINK TANK

FEVER, DREAM   114
"LEAVE LIQUIDS HERE" — TSA   116
A PIECE OF LIFE   117
FUNERAL CEREMONY AS PARADE   120
WHEN ANYONE DIES   121
WHAT'S IN A DAY   122
LIFE   123
ESCAPES   124
DREW   127

A New Distraction *128*
Command for my Past *129*
This is What I See *130*
Escapes II *132*
If I Could Mail-Order Him *133*
After I Lock the Front Door *134*

IV. No Matter the Wreckage

Night Walking *138*
Numb Days *141*
Broken Umbrellas *142*
The Rush to the Bicycle *143*
Under Winter *144*
If I were a Book *145*
Alden's French Tulips *146*
The Anniversary of Her Escape *149*
As a Child *150*
My Mother *151*
The Mind-Path of a Child *152*
The Potential Energy of a Child *155*
Ride Home From The Blue Fish Restaurant, 2007 *156*

A Daydream *157*
Autobiography of a House *158*
5G *159*
Train from Rome to Florence *160*

V. Then Winter & The Tulip-Flame

September 7th *164*
Cold Front *165*
Surroundings *166*
Play *167*
Timeline of Tuesday From a Child's Perspective *168*
9th Street *169*
Daylight Savings *170*
After a Poetry Reading *171*
For the Holidays *172*
A String of Days That Ends with Light *175*
Arriving Home *176*
At the Bus Stop *177*
Found Item I Will Use for a Stereognostic Mystery Bag *178*

EXAM PREPARATION *179*
NIGHT RUN IN MARKET SQUARE *180*
ON MY WAY TO THE BOOKSTORE *183*
PHOTOGRAPH OF MY MOTHER'S MORNING WALK (1998) *184*
LOVE AT FIRST SIGHT *185*
HAVEN FROM STALKER / JOURNAL FROM HOTEL *186*
THE IN-BETWEEN DAYS *189*
SUNSET *190*
MORNING DEW *191*
GARDENING *192*
NOTES FROM A NEW STATE *195*
THE ILLNESS OF BEAUTY *196*
ON THE ANNIVERSARY OF MY ESCAPE *197*
WHAT IF EVERYTHING WASN'T A LIE *198*
ABOUT SILENCE *199*
SHE WAS HAPPY *200*
LETTER TO GOD *203*
TO SEE YOU *204*
TRYST *205*
THE ENCOUNTER *206*
PASSING THE PATISSERIE *207*
HOLIDAY DRIZZLE *208*

DEPRESSION HOUR *209*
THE CURE *210*
IN MY DREAM OF US *213*
WHAT WE'LL SHARE *214*
BRUSH *215*
LET YOURSELF BE LOVED *216*
AIRPORT ROSES *217*
LOVE'S BEGINNING *218*
WHAT WE HAVE *221*
CHAPMAN DRIVE *222*
POND LILY *223*
DECEMBER 9TH *224*
MORCEAU DE TEMPS *225*
A NOTICING *226*
I COME HOME TO *229*
ANOTHER BURNING OF ESTES PARK *230*
HOW THIS BOOK WAS MADE *231*

ACKNOWLEDGEMENTS *233*
REVIEWS *235*
NOTES *237*

I. Life of the Party

*"Everything has either already happened
or never will."*
— *Olivia Gatwood*

Before Television
with select words from Olivia Gatwood's "All of the Missing Girls Are Hanging Out With Us"

in a field   in a river   under tall grass
in a park or a drained pond   in the living room
who can catch the most gold-amber light
through the glass windows   sun on the walls
chestnut-colored & coated in honey   broken
by our human hands   a kaleidoscope
of moments dances until dark   when sleep will carry
our gentle bodies   like doves   into the night

The Dog

with select words from Olivia Gatwood's "Ode to the Women on Long Island"

I draw on a window with my fingerpad before Christmas, watching snow hills bunch up against each other.

A black and gingerbread ball sprawls through the glittering dusk.

After dark, I call her in. Her body circles me on the rug and settles like a blossom in its threads.

Snowflakes are a cherry on top of her nose. They melt away like I do in her brown sugar eyes.

I comb the pine needles out of my hair, then hers.

She shuffles around in my shams,* stretching and circling the fabric like it's bubblegum.

On the side of my house, in the basement, by the couch, trudging through the snowmelt — she's there wherever I go, a hero just for being.

---

*Sham — a pillow case.

Highschool & Then

with select words from Olivia Gatwood's "The Boy Says He Loves Ted Bundy but Doesn't Laugh About It" & page 59

Neither the boy in the butter-yellow sweater — not quite a hot-shot scholar of girls — nor the boy who likes cheap beer and a party will sit up in their chairs. They hide, hunch their backs, and sometimes perk up to see a pair of shiny legs.

After school, the boy who likes cheap beer and a party switches lips with a skinny girl that blows cigarette smoke in between kisses. The boy in the butter-yellow sweater sits on the grass and won't place my hand on his. I pull the daisies like taffy and ask him why the sky is blue. I'm afraid of him and my cheek he won't kiss, but I dream about him anyway.

GIRLS

> *with select words from Olivia Gatwood's "My Mother's Addendum" & "Body Count: 13"*

Exactly how can a girl's mind rehearse, *I'm not afraid,* when she gave him a secret?
It subtracts from her.

Two people continue to not find more in each other.
Dependence, emptiness.
This is how he loves her — until he doesn't anymore.

Anyone on the wrong side of the wait — the chase — gathers dust. And then, maybe, a quick, lucky escape.

Some Men

> *with select words from Olivia Gatwood's "I Am Almost Certain I Could Dispose of Myself and Get Away With It"*

Some men love the cleanup.
If a girl can be found dying,
one of them will take her in.
Some men will lift her crepe skin
and wear it.

The one who's chosen me
finds me full of death.
It's what makes him begin with me
in the first place.
He unsews my skin, and I love it.
It's what makes him leave, too.

He gives it back after
it's been emptied, gives it back
to no one.

I find a remnant of myself
and sew a cover on it.
I wrap myself in peach and no one.
Now, I am more.

LET HER LIVE

with select words from Olivia Gatwood's "Aileen Wuornos Takes a Lover Home"

Take a lover. Promise to let her breathe.
Say she'll be listened to.

Love her right arm and her neck.
Love the pale girl who drinks

whiskey and wears red.
Love every version of her

smile. And each time,
let her live.

BREAKFAST
with select words from Olivia Gatwood's "A Story Ending in Breakfast"

I

I draw a boy
After staying up all night
With nobody

I talk to myself
Over my pencil's vibrations
This morning

I make you for breakfast
Opposite me at the table
You look comfortable

I imagine us talking
I want to tell you
About my body

I want you to understand
How I must make a ritual
Out of habit

Some people need coffee
Or a cigarette
I need love and its habits

II

The middle of winter is soon
The rush of Desire
Passes the time

The boy's body becomes a gift
I dream of it in my hands
Like a velvet box

Form a simple habit, I tell him
Take me with you again and again
He does — of course he does

I unsew myself in preparation
For when he comes to me
With his hand on my shoulder

As he always will
A vibrant thread of light
That illuminates my future

He's merely a dream with a face
In my vision
He tends to my torn palms

With wrapping cloth
Imagination is just that
A tending to torn parts of the mind

The Agreement

with select words from Olivia Gatwood's "The Lover as a Dream"

a line of sun lays over a garden gate while
champagne rain pours. he wants a picture;
we lean together. i want to dance
for a crowd of my new, bright lover.
maybe i'll drop the idea of an agreement
if he drops "yes" from the same location:
doubt/fear. the water grows. *conversation* —
there's progress here. his thumb sweeps
a raindrop from my bottom lip. i want
to stay. we are not yet lovers, but
a stone bench holds us together.

The Other Side of Brokenness
with select words from Olivia Gatwood's "Ode to my Lover's Left Hand"

On our first night, he admits what he knows and what he doesn't. Suddenly, ordinary becomes a miracle; romance becomes his right hand over the map of me. He swims to the bottom of Brokenness. "Open; breathe until you reach sea level," he says. "Learn that blooming is easy." But what is being alive? What is light? It's my lover's voice unlocking my throat. He loses his breath somewhere in mine. When I come up, which side am I on? Land and sea have combined. Now, my inside is the sky, a home for him.

Saturday Morning

with select words from Olivia Gatwood's "The Lover as Corn Syrup"

The syrup comes.

"You must stay," I say.

I keep my lover as the reason behind everything I crave:

Someone sitting, something I consume.

Both settle in my belly.

I hold my middle.

A Little, Dark Evening
with select words from Olivia Gatwood's "I Am Always Trying To Make my Poems Timeless"

I talk to myself in the library.
Lighter than a star, I think,
I've found the man I'm prettier with.

A lilac dress on his doorstep, I'm relieved
I am finally here. I haven't reached for perfect —
only a little dark evening with a slip of promise.

Through the house to the backyard,
we don't take too long.
Soon, we're in a tree.

Fireflies are small moons around us.
He stamps my cheek with lips
that are cold-brushed by the wind.

Let me have so many hours.
Fall in love with me.
He is capable of everything.

If I'll Smile for Anyone
with select words from Olivia Gatwood's "Ode To Pink"

Color is: to swallow you in pink bites.

Your voice, your words — something I learn.

You feel like a fresh piece of bubblegum: hot and new.

You're a fabulous coat.

If I could, I would coat my whole body in a layer of you.

Sliced grapefruit and rosé smear across my dainty throat.

For you, I'll smile.

CAPTURE
with select words from Olivia Gatwood's "My Girl"

Outside his window: rolling silver clouds —
still, long, easy, & tied around her neck.

She rides the high note of his bedpost,
remembering how he found her in the mud.

He watches the girl & holds her.

"I'm not going to let anybody hurt us."

Thin Cotton

> *with select words from Olivia Gatwood's "The Lover as a Cult"*

I am an ankle-length, cotton dress hanging thin.
You watch over me as I blow in the wind.
How do I hold that feeling — the cusp of spring?

I remember April's laundry. You praised the way I hung and folded. I laid out on the field and fell asleep in the breeze before you draped my body over a wire. You admired how everything becomes new, even me for you.

Outside, I hang myself over the vision of your hands. I practice wringing my neck to dry faster, but my hands are just holes.

A piece of my laced edge blows by me. My hemline has come undone.

Heart of Many Colors II*
with select words from Olivia Gatwood's "Mans/Laughter"

Before sleep, my lover's red laugh lodges itself in my lungs.
Our breathing patterns struggle. We drift away, out of each
other's arms.

At once, he leaves the bed. The room becomes a heavy net. I
watch him over the balcony.

Out on the porch, he stares into a black evening.
This man, woken by pain, is more like a boy reaching out his
fingers in the dark. He can't swallow his past, so he laughs.

I sit next to him on the porch's cold stones.
He doesn't say hello.

We return to the bedroom. We sleep.

At sunrise, we find a bakery, swinging our coupled hands in
the morning air. He mentions how he'd like to hold on to me
without killing himself.

We seat ourselves with our treats. He isn't hungry as I peel off
a croissant's buttered top. Our eyes exchange both the delight
of each other's company and the deeper dread of life.

He says, "It's hard to smile most of the time. I smile for you,
because I don't want to be too dark."* I place my hand in his
and stuff a new layer of croissant into my mouth.

*See "Heart of Many Colors" in *Elizabeth Young: The Mind's Mess*.
*Lines from "Too Dark" in *Elizabeth Young: The Mind's Mess*.

Find Him

with select words from Olivia Gatwood's "When They Find Him"

Love him, but expect his hiding.
He will hide from you, from
feeling, from his pain. Turn East;
turn golden; light him up. Be
a warm, vanilla-filled home. Catch
his wondering look across a room.

A Dark House
with select words from Olivia Gatwood's "Ode to the Unpaid Electricity Bill"

My lover is selectively distant.

He lets my letters sit abandoned.

I hope he calls or

is delivered to my doorstep.

One morning, I woke to his call

and apologized profusely

for every crime I'd never committed.

Every day after that has been a dark house

searching for light. But what is light

if not his constant hum?

Now, I sit in the dark while my phone battery dwindles,

not yet knowing that he won't return

no matter how much I voice my love.

He calls, and I lay there forever, listening to him

apologize profusely every crime he's ever committed.

My lover tells me he tried his best,

but it's a lie.

To Someone Who Isn't
with select words from Olivia Gatwood's "Sonnet for the Clove of Garlic Inside Me"

yesterday i broke against my twisted knees

evening   skinned knuckles

you   working overtime

i take your thick poison

you know it works

swallow me again

The Bad Boy
with select words from Olivia Gatwood's "Eubank & Candelaria, 2009"

When he speaks, sparks fly off his tongue. They land on me, crackling, glittering, leaving marks. He grips my arm. His strength is terrifying and beautiful, his words inconsistent and delicate. He kisses me and says I cause more trouble than anything else.

★

The stars rise. He doesn't answer my calls. I unlock his front door. He is gone.

★

This morning, the sun matches the Hawaiian volcanoes. My mind spins itself into infinite paths. Some paths lead to his disappearance, some to his return, some to our wedding, others into a crater.

★

I decide to walk. Out by the volcanoes, lava bubbles burst and hiss. They sound like cowboys with lassos. Their rumblings remind me of his voice. Wherever I go, I sense his absence and ache with a nostalgia that will never be satisfied. Wherever I go, he is the Wild West, missing for years.

How a Girl Dies

      with select words from Olivia Gatwood's "Say It, I'm Always
                                             in Love" and "2041"

Girl   "Let's look into the rising sun,
          into the gradient horizon.
          Your chest is where my head goes.
          We are tulip trees* with yellow* leaves.
          Don't let this winter frost us to death.
          Soon, a door will open for you.
          Soon, a new horizon will surface.
          These leaves will turn over, and
          you'll be in spring again."

Boy   "I'm dry and frozen. I have no yellow leaves.
          The horizon is gray, speckled with dust
          from the nation. I wither. My chest
          has sunken in, and I can't hold you up
          any longer. These remnants of life
          will expire soon. There will be no more
          springs for me and you."

          No one believes I lost these six minutes
          in a parking lot. I thought that by winter,
          by spring, by next fall, he would be the way
          I lived. Now, I know this is how a girl dies.

---

*Tulip trees have an exceptional life span of four to five centuries.
*Yellow — a color scientifically proven to make people happy.

Lover's Quarrel
with select words from Olivia Gatwood's "The Scholar"

"To me, the sea lives in your sound," she says.

He asks for a large bag, begs her.

"Love me," she says, giving over the bag.

Silence.

The gate swings.

Her house is morning fog.

PTSD on September 2nd
with select words from Olivia Gatwood's "My Grandmother Asks Why I Don't Trust Men"

My father and I, alone with our breath, walk an empty trail.

A slow ghost floats in front of me but doesn't respond to my interactions with it.

Around a corner, a biker stretches against a tree.

To me, it's *him* stretching against a tree.

I can't unlove him, I think. I stare at the ghost.

My father grabs my shoulders to shake parts of *him* loose.

"Show and tell the dark times," he says. "Maybe the worst is the parade of memories."

I will. But sometimes, I search for his name behind my front door or in a jar of flowers. Even in an elevator while the void of me crimps under a jazz song.

Tell, Tell
> *with select words from Olivia Gatwood's "Will I Ever Stop*
> *Writing About the Dead Girl" & page 104*

He's gone, but maybe he'll come back — maybe
if he hears my name, he'll change.

He once loved, tumbled, & turned me
into small parts by the land.

I'm sorry you hung on so long.
Write it down. Choose a paint color.

Take some pictures on your walk. Braid
your hair. Dwell on what inspires you,

and joy will come. Tell people
how it happened. Stand on your truth.

COURT

with select words from Olivia Gatwood's "What I Know About Healing"

The story was so full,

Was bubbling over like molasses.

I ran to get a bucket.

I caught every memory in it,

Told the court what happened,

Dropped the bucket,

Stepped in the molasses,

Cried prisms.

Worn From War
with select words from Olivia Gatwood's "Ode To My Jealousy"

Now, I glitter with slashes and blood;
    my cuts are curtains worn from war.

In every sore, you appear,
    somehow still what I adore.

I try to close them,
    but you are there.

Your coat of shards in my open arms:
    tiny mirrors that split me apart,

shimmering thorns carved deep
    in my heart.

My emerald prayers, frail and short,
    were defenseless against your silver words.

You vanished and ignored my bones on the floor.
    You left my middle open and bare.

If only these wounds were fixed with stitches,
    the scars would emerge like brittle stars,

and I'd be draped in two satin sashes,
    one of tears and one, a memoir.

A Good Story

> *with select words from Olivia Gatwood's "To my Favorite Murder"*

one day, i can't place my heart —
it's missing. my lost dream of living
shapeshifts into a footstep's sound,
into boots in a hallway, into a man.

i've always wanted a man, but every time,
my heart fractures, red & cracked open.
still, i imagine castles in the air,
piecing her back together with feelings
i can't hold in my dress pockets.

i'm not alive, i'm just a good story.
maybe this page is just when it happened,
when i became it, & it became me.

BLACK WINTER

with select words from Olivia Gatwood's "Here Is What You Need To Know"

To resurrect from a black winter,
You must tumble into bruising water.
You must swim to get out.
The ice will hold you there, nearer than *he* ever did,
And the cabins will hear you thrashing.
Your legs will come up floating like the dead,
But there is a sign by the river:

The best woman takes the water
Even though it slices through her.

Swim the bruises out.
Leave the water.
Hold yourself until you are warm.
Let your legs defrost.
Accept the black winter,
And never let yourself be found in another.
The air around you is not intended to be
Thick and loud.
Let us see your face again.

Lines for Turning Aspens
with select words from Olivia Gatwood's "Another Thing I Know About Healing"

somewhere between
remembering
what i'd said to you last
and the window's blur
my car passed a family
of burgundy trees
i saw them and shook

Death of a Once-Loved One
with select words from Olivia Gatwood's "The Lover as Tapeworm" & page 74

Before sleep, how heavy it is to be alive.
How heavy is the bittersweet song of doors
that swing open with the draft after you're gone.
Their creaking presses old wounds in my sternum
from the doors that would swing and scream
and sing when you touched them, shoved them,
rushed through them. I remember your sinking eyes,
how they held open like doors by brief moments
of will and wind. How heavy it is to have lived.

After I've Died

*with select words from Olivia Gatwood's "Sound Bites While
We Ponder Death"*

A recycled-cotton sundress catches
on a twig.

A young girl pauses in the breeze
and looks over her shoulder,
hoping to find someone there.

The sound of my absence
bites as she walks through
the shadows of oak leaves.

White noise is her new guardian.
Her desire for my company
doesn't end.

She walks through me
between the swaying trees.

My daughter searches the shadows,
the spaces where I used to hold her hand.

Passerby

with select words from Olivia Gatwood's Life of the Party,
page 95

I see you peek through
her warped doorframe.
Your mind fills in
the broken images
with what you think
you want to know.
You leave her porch
combing splinters
from your hair.
On to the next house.

Funeral for a Twenty-Something
with select words from Olivia Gatwood's "She Lit Up Every Room She Walked Into"

On her face was everyone she'd ever met.
Did you hear that a smile made her
that much more desirable? I heard
a girl's bright eye can never disappoint the world,
almost like the blue sky with its silver lining
that clutches the fence, its cream cushions,
and soft music that we sing to.

NIGHT-RIVER
with select words from Olivia Gatwood's "The Summer of 2008 at Altura Park"

From the corner of the most hidden tree,
I pull a handful of silence.

The forest looks at me.
It whispers, "I got you something."

I sit down in the sponge-grass
and weave my fingers

together in my lap, knitting
the part of the river that disappears

into the rest of the night.
I wait for it to unfold.

How to Seize the Day
with select words from Olivia Gatwood's Life of the Party, *page 140*

don't skip over a full day   here's a clue

there's a whole evening left   watch its light play

in your hands   on the floor   out the door

hold   a rose's tanned thorn   run her petals down

a foggy window   hum a crescendo*

★Crescendo — the loudest point reached in a gradually increasing sound.

The Jacket

> *with select words from Part I of Olivia Gatwood's* Life of the Party

October 13, 2020 —
A little jacket lies on its back, naked
in the dirt. Through cracked twigs
and stacked leaf blades, yellow poppies
litter a small label, just pressed, like currency.

This belongs on an October slide,
singing a burgundy pitch so gentle,
any pain is blown to confetti, I think.

I remember an October afternoon in 2002 —

A rose-colored form billows, draped,
loose as a duvet, over a branch, quiet
except for the crinkle of aspen leaves
in a breeze that spills from autumn's glass.

Pockets of envy under my dress demand
that my tiny hands bunch its cotton,
my legs to unfold in front of me,
dictating my anticipated grip around the jacket.

I am glass-eyed & yellow-minded.
It is noon. My buttercream dress doesn't lose
a tenth of a second. A small howl &
heavy breath hang loose over the branch.

Swirling, disoriented in my own forest,
I return to my address, face speckled red.

My front door seems nervous
& unwilling to close. I don't feel safe
in the kitchen, so I scale the perimeter.
The floorboards whine, splintering me
with interrogation. I hurdle fourteen stair steps
to shake loose the first floor's suspicion.

After strawberry season, I grow dizzy
that I took a small girl's coat,
her sweet spoon of crystal sugar.
With each day's passing, it looks
more like rotting figs, a dying flame,
her pile of sadness. The width
of something worshiped by someone
blisters my insides with its hard corners.

The small girl must sob into her pillow
at wanting it home. She might give anything
for the smallest crumb of time reversal,
seven minutes even, to coax her
coat back, to watch it tumble
in her mother's washing machine, to feel
its lined cuffs bunch around her knuckles
while she holds a Halloween sparkler.

The myth of desire burns out. I toss her
soft, bitter skin into the dirt. A rolling sun
plummets, my watermelon tongue, chewed.

Eighteen years and sun after sun
have muted its sterling ribbons,
and, just near its side, a purple fungus
peers, soundless, over its unzipped stomach.

Bear Crossing
with select words from Olivia Gatwood's "Ode to My Bitch Face"

A bulbous head sways over the road.
Little bulbs follow her under constellations.

Pink tongues taste the ground between
Streetlights: a foreign language to theirs.

While they rest under the moon,
We call them monsters,

Panic at the sight of them, scream
At a family just crossing by.

All this while their bodies become
White flags some mornings, many nights.

How can they sleep when
Their home is our construction zone,

Their safe place, our asphalt road?
It's not the forest that decorates

Our mountain drive, but the drive
That plows through their mountainside.

Boulder, Colorado
with select words from Olivia Gatwood's "Aileen Wuornos Convinces Me to Put Down My Dog"

Accept this city, a chunk
in the shape of the state.

Scoop it with a spoon.
At the mall, try on all
the peach pressed pants.

Read on a blanket.
Protect your house,
so old you must carry
her up the stairs.

Be somewhere where
they give you exotic coffee.
Enjoy something —
a whole chicken.
Rip it to shreds.

The Grind
with select words from Olivia Gatwood's "Elegy for Allegedly"

Write, drink, sleep.
Pill, pen, pill, pen.
It rains and blows while I scribble.
The pattern repeats itself.

WHAT CAPITALISM DEMANDS
with select words from Olivia Gatwood's "Aileen Wuorno Isn't My Hero"

Do you know how to pull, grip, shout, swear?

Be cold & foaming for success.

Stop. Go. Work, already.

Build an eight-foot-high fence.

Move, change, run, have too many friends.

Be religious about absolutely everything — jewelry, spoons, every dollar, nicotine — but don't identify as such.

Buy land until your properties number like mist droplets.

Wish all these people loved you.

Grasp whatever victory means for you until it's too hard, then look for something easier.

Drink too much. Be impulsive; face the screens.

Be the kind who can't listen.

Be pushed, jump; be easy on purpose.

Become the people.

Think I'm a great candidate.

Love watching my chair from behind.

Love international cities.

Need this, that. Be there, here.

Give a good quote. Always be lying.

Be impatient — you're always behind.

Neglect relationships; make excuses.

Tear down The White Castle.

Eat cake. Have a party. Ditch it to go smoke on The White Castle's lawn.

Know how to have fun, to flirt.

Stop asking questions.

Tell me no one is watching, then broadcast everything.

Simple Pleasures From 1935 to Now
with select words from Olivia Gatwood's "In the Future, I Love the Nighttime"

A spring breeze over a cup of tea. / River water moving. / An ink-papered read. / A drawer of pillows — sleep. / Oysters, silver and wet. / The science of sound. / The melodic word, "cornflower." / The parts of a little house that grow bigger with sunlight. / Colors when dipped in each other. / Novels begging for a tender touch. / The good spell of a man with a bullfrog throat. / Laughing heads at parties with quick flashes of all our alternate lives. / A climb toward blue and you. / Chests quiet as a balloon. / The days I still have memories. / The burnt bottom of a dedicated lightbulb. / All we have now are stones, the ground, & a trail of carnelian* lives. / The mirror wrestles. I back down.

---

*Carnelian — a vibrant, energetic gemstone thought by some to inspire a zest for life and tap into one's power and creativity. It comes in shades that vary from pale orange to dark reddish-brown.

II. Behind My Eyes

"Wait for evening. Then you'll be alone."
— *Li-Young Lee*

Things We Don't Make Time to Imagine
with select words from Li-Young Lee's "Sweet Peace And Time"

What if days go by, and you comb the knots
out of the sea, turn them into apple blossoms,
carve through nights and days, and place
some in the ground? What if time is sifted,
if laughter rocks the trees and fetches wings
from each blossom, sending butterflies over
the range of emerald hills that hold me?
What if the wind in the trees is the sound
of the East changing its pajamas? And Death
is a secret, a first and last place, no place at all,
a home but not a house? What if, long before
the world, there was just the color blue?

Before Punctuation

with select words from Li-Young Lee's "Dying Stupid"

Day is broken by Night: a thread
skipping through a field.
Cornstalks toss their pollen tassels
toward the shadows of recent flowers.
Each evening, sentences play,
clinging to notions of freedom
under the scattered voices of thunder.
Imperfect word orders
create mysteries of disappearance
while birds make shadow puppets
in the moonlight.

Autumn

> *with select words from Li-Young Lee's "Lake Effect"*

Withering rains pepper her satin wilderness
with rainbow leaves. Mountain Bluebirds
weave their nests out of the stars of her season.
In her language of colors, she commands
the forests' green ribbons to untie. Autumn's
cellophane winds open doors, pull coat buttons,
sweep little ponds into a spiral. She tumbles
into September, scuffing the mountains' knees —
they burst red. Wonder: the sound of her aspens
putting on their new dresses. But, each year,
fire erases Autumn's genesis. The mountains'
blushing changes to bleeding, then eschar,* and
the silver sky covers her, a distant memory.

*Eschar — pervasive, necrotic tissue resulting from a burn injury.

A November Week

with select words from Li-Young Lee's "My Favorite Kingdom"

monday rain & a cloud of bees

      a tuesday window looks onto the various stages of
                                  the storm's end

   wednesday begins   a book whose every page is
a long way from home

     thursday to friday   the arms of my favorite door
                                       receive me

saturday swings from thanksgiving noons   to sunday

                    my door's brass knob almost turns
                                  a thousand times

A Sunday Afternoon on the Island of La Grand Jatte, Georges Seurat, 1884

with select words from Li-Young Lee's "My Clothes Lie Folded for the Journey"

Folded rain sleeps. I part its mane and enter
the dance of the living. The shadows of The Gates
of Meeting and Parting tell the time. My heart
faces the sun, displayed to a hidden world
of Anyone Can Read Who Knows the Language.
I pause to find a boy reading and searching.
As he reads, the pages fall through his fingers,
making the sound of water walking beside
a river's bank. I sit down, arrange my feet to face
his blanket, and sew. I wouldn't be afraid to fold
my blanket over onto his, to lie down by him,
to sew him a new one if he asked me to.

Man With No Bags

with select words from Li-Young Lee's "Station"

"Your attention, please." The announcement blankets us, every passenger that waits. Waiting makes itself into various shapes around the airport. Waiting sits on a suitcase; Waiting leans against a wall. "Excuse me, is this seat taken?" On my left side, a new type of Waiting stations himself. This Waiting has a camouflage uniform and no bags.

Meeting him stills me. *Your name is at either end of Rescue. You either need it or perform it*, I think. Dazed in my seat, I consider the possibility of his name in my mouth and mine in his.

Suddenly, I imagine falling petals and his attention, pink clouds, seafoam, and leisure. From hibernation, an ancient happiness unfolds within me, then a carnation field, then a sunrise. Finally, the sea herself arrives out of hidden ground.

My baggage was heavy before you and might be heavier after you, but this is my full heart's song asking for your approach — *your attention, please.*

When the Man Falls into a Trap
with select words from Li-Young Lee's "In His Own Shadow"

She draws light from the sun,   spins it into an aura
        she carries with her day and night:
    to some radiance,   to others, a fire.

Over time, she darkens, but he writes
        her loveliness into being,   reversing the truth.

He draws light over her hatred for him   to lift
    the ever-rising dusk   that hovers over him.

She is the first darkness
        within the lighter dark of dusk   around him.

With time,   two lights bend: his mind
        and the white moon in his hand.

One makes it difficult to see two steps ahead,
     and the other keeps him
         from acknowledging his own Death — her.

How Could You Not Want to Save Him
with select words from Li-Young Lee's "Living With Her"

A brown house holds him: young and yet, old.
His audible aches make me think his voice is a wheel
rolling uphill. What he doesn't say walks around his eyes
to make crow's feet. The years that sleep behind him
wake up and yawn occasionally, but they settle again.
After exhausting my hand scribbling observations,
I build my river beside his house and consider him
in the low-light hour. He gazes at nothing through
the glass. *Come away from the window. Sit down,* I think.
*There's no dark out there that isn't first in you. Come sit
by the river with me. We can sail, swim, wade, or drink.
I'll let you choose.* What a narrow existence he has.
If only the glass would come down from his eyes
so he could see the river and the gold-coin, aspen leaves.

Talking Parker Down From the Bar Counter
with select words from Li-Young Lee's "Have You Prayed"

Do you have a voice?
Speak to me.

I know it's only one wish
Between rapture or breath,
Branch or wand, death or life.
Have you ever given
A winter fire more wood
Or a dream more time?

The embers in you look dim,
But they still burn.
There is joy in you;
There is passion and love.

But do you have a voice?
Use that instead of a glass —
Pull the poison out, pearls first.

NOVEMBER 7TH AFTER RIDING THE WIND ALL THE WAY HOME
with select words from Li-Young Lee's "Fire Enthroned"

Against a wall, your eyes splash me like a watercolor bloom,* calling me urgently into your buttoned chest. "Not another word," you whisper. *Pick up my heart from the cold floor, woven of dust and yearning,* I think. You trace the vertical lines of my body — your fingers are matches, sparking a fire in each rod that holds me together. The lapsed echoes of my damage stack into a hunger for your pressure. I push my lips together, but you pull them apart, keeping score of how many times you do. Overhead, Edison bulbs look at us through their glasses and tie us up with strings of orange light. Your tongue tastes of spring water, your body a bed of leaves against me. There's no cold place this autumn, not since we blew in.

The hot wind around us brushes open a September door to the ocean, and you take me around the corner. My plea for you changes pitch the faster we go. Like seashells, you collect each plea for miles as we tumble down the beach. You look for them, for louder calls in the pleats of my parched lips, never satisfied. Your desire is boundless and ambitious, forging its path without caring who watches. By sunrise, our linens are drying on the hedges, casting a shadow, and we're asking the shorebirds to watch over our things.

---

*Watercolor bloom — noun describing how pigment spreads when added to a droplet of water.

The Heart
with select words from Li-Young Lee's "The Apple Elopes"

By repetition, I learn the heart.
She is not a forgetful flesh.
She is sweet and round.
She steeps in her memories.
Her tone sounds bitter at times,
Warning me from the edge of the yard
Not to be too spontaneous.
She asks of my ripening
And the growing shade
Over yesterday's decisions
From the porch stairs.
She waits for me to come to my senses
As she brushes the tangles
From my better judgment.

Connection

with select words from Li-Young Lee's "To Hold"

We hold opposite edges
of a billowing pull between us.

We tug, gather, tuck. We lie down,
and it gets harder to let go.

One day, we will surrender all we guard.
Until then, we take what isn't for our having,

dream, and abandon Time. This pull
is a joint and fragile keeping.*

---

*Keeping — something that is kept.

Trapping a Magic Feeling

> *with select words from Li-Young Lee's "A Hymn To Childhood"*

There's a hymn that doesn't last: any feeling so euphoric that you can't, in goodwill, let her go. So, you board her up in the attic, that magic Feeling which once strolled the streets around you, weaving a certain air. Is a hidden feeling still felt?

You walk past your attic each dawn to visit, then abandon, the magic Feeling. You learn to view her from the safety of the door's sliver where the draft crawls through. You move like a ghost around your home, turning over China cups with porcelain fingers so as not to scare her.

Winter comes, and on that day, you open a letter, one that bursts the magic Feeling into small confetti, words that poison her oxygen with Despair. Gravity pulls her limp remains through the dusted slats of the attic's vents. She lands piece by piece, disappearing into the snow.

Now, when you hear the wind in the roof slats, the dove's melody in the evening, or take in the unseen morning, Bitterness peels your rusted lips. From here to the beginning of any magic Feeling just as strong, you'll mourn the winter that holds her in its glittering capsules.

Afternoon Nap to Kill Time
with select words from Li-Young Lee's "Seven Happy Endings"

You, happy after talking all night, meant to call today.
But something — maybe shadows on the garden wall —

stopped you, a man rowing alone out to sea.
I divide daylight waiting for you to act.

I divide it with the knife of house chores
and mail opening. Bells from down the street

make me wish for you more. I rest;
missing you is exhausting. I dream

That you row alone out to sea.
My dream-spirit slips into the ocean.

On the other side of the mountains
where you row, you dip your eyes

below the ocean's line and see my spirit reaching
for your face through the sunbeams.

My hand stretches out for yours when your oars
kiss the water. Suddenly, a word is spoken

over our whole world: "Genevieve."
The lips of rocks around us echo

the word over and over. Its letters fall
from the sky. Gathering the overspilled

characters with my eyelashes, I force my eyes
to lift them, heavy. "Genevieve, Genevieve."

I wake to my own voice. I turn over
to see the moon rise on your disappearance.

WHEN HE LEFT
with select words from Li-Young Lee's "The Lives of a Voice:
1. Dear and With"

he let go of an outstretched hand,
of several worlds the day he left.
fear and desire became one.
dreams and appetite divorced
and devoured my wild eyes,
leaving desolation.
desolation hatched,
multiplied —
one bird became many,
became fractured glass inside me.
i began to confuse fear and desire,
misinterpret dreams for appetite,
mistake the crinkled wings of my ambition
for every time a man touched me.
it was in these moments
that my lifetime of longing commenced.

Her Second Sigh

> *with select words from Li-Young Lee's "Virtues of the Boring Husband"*

I pass a pale girl, old as a quarter's worth, dangled on a park bench. She lets out one sigh, then another.

Maybe her second sigh is a sigh for the whole universe, or perhaps it's the lack of love ringing out from an uncontainable place within her. It might be an expression of surrender or the crowning experience of someone else's mistake. Maybe she's the host of that confusion.

I ask her what it's for — her second sigh. "For him," she says. "If I remember correctly, love is discovering the deeper aspects of ourselves and tying a knot. He and I were once tying knots around the edges of a winter blanket. But he cut the threads and ran."

In My Story, He Stays
with select words from Li-Young Lee's "The Shortcut Home"

Two winds breathe, fanning my feet as I hike on coals from
yesterday's fires — summer in the Rockies.

In my story, birds sing to me from the highest branch
of the origin of hours if all timelines were a tree.

In my story, I find God's coat hiding in
the apple trees, under the hills' grass blankets,
in the first mouthful of wildfire smoke and the last.

In my story, I have a stone path I follow back to sleep:
kisses grown into straw, straw fused into a sign that points
the way, and a donkey to carry me down to His kind hand
that will give me rest.

In my story, I bring a man through my white, wooden door,
and he stays.

Long Lake
with select words from Li-Young Lee's "Lake Effect"

November 15, 8:34pm, Long Lake —

I sit by Long Lake, my loyal companion. A sunset finds its way to other hands, turning shadows of clouds into shadows of waves. In silent tumult, birds and leaves blow to the other side of Earth. The lake is a blanket — fresh linen — folding over itself with each figure of unsalted foam. It changes its mind between the laws of water and wind until it tires itself out, laying flat.

Dark is the song of every leap I take to find Joy. Each one makes a thick wedge in the charcoal sand. As I walk, my steps dissolve into laughter, and the lake hides them in its hands. Joy braids her pale gold hair on a high ledge. I leap over the lake to close the gap between her and me, but I land hard on the jagged edges of a cliff's side. I grasp for Joy's crystal shelf as I drop, but Grief's weather-beaten foot pushes off each finger unforgivingly. Hostages seen only by the moon's brief glimmer, my efforts to reach Joy drag into the clear fire of morning.

November 16, 5:33am, Long Lake —

The lake-linen ruffles, unrolling over the horizon. Foam figures lie toppled and confused on the rocky shore. Vermillion welts pollute my fair skin. I immerse my legs in the tired foam, changing places with Striving for a moment. But the world comes after me and grabs the foam from around my ankles. A new wind blows the microscopic bubbles up into the air. I rise to salvage some in my worn fingers but return with only space as they fly away.

November 16, 7:01am, Long Lake —

The lake doubles over and creases. The indefinite future of my struggles whitens with the fattening spread of dawn.

Nonna Sews a New Wall-Hanging
with select words from Li-Young Lee's "Lake Effect"

Sewing a blanket of fleeting ships, she said,
"The cloud's shadows tell a story."

She said, "My sewn clouds, in this boundless space,
turn toward each other to form a storm."

"Who's running down here in the rain?" I asked.
"You," she said.

She pushed the silver needle. "Now, I'm filling the Beyond
with shifting shades of blue."

She said, "Do you see me? Do you see the space
between our bodies?"

"Barely a hand, hardly a breath, because
I'm always running in the rain with you."

She said, "This ocean is the beginning of happiness
if you can make your mind swim out into it."

She said, "Sit by an open window at dawn. Listen to
the doves through the ragged seasons."

Sun Salutation
with select words from Li-Young Lee's "Becoming Becoming"

i wait for evening to empty   when my closed eyes

become a hiding place   i don't forget to listen while i sleep

i wait for a gold wind's story through my window-screen

i stray into the woods   in search of the growing hands

behind all of time   i travel with the leaves   trade places

with the wind   remember light   wake to the morning

What Matters
with select words from Li-Young Lee's "Self-Help for a Fellow Refugees" and "Mother Deluxe"

what matters is your favorite spoon, the first card

in a new deck, the 20th century, pure-pressed olive oil.

what matters is what's on the side of the road, rescue,

depending on our blood to keep us living. what matters

is the world evening news, mystery, depth of thought,

having a good boat, any night with you, the rest of my life.

Hiding Until Love Asks That She Comes Out to Play
with select words from Li-Young Lee's "Living With Her 2."

She counts the months
and days. One evening,
she emerges. She is
a pomegranate entirely
beginning to sweeten.

CREATION STORY
with select words from Li-Young Lee's "The Mother's Apple"

Pockets spill out of the wind, each holding
a key, unlocking a blossom. Each blossom
becomes a bee; a map; a piano; a shipwreck;

a star somewhere; my ancestry; a Pink Pearl
apple tree; unimaginable winters; heavy tears;
the planet; a fourfold mystery; bitterness,

skin deep that, for some, can't be helped;
my sweetening that draws me nearer and
nearer that apple tree.

Asking the Moon About my Husband
with select words from Li-Young Lee's "The Father's Apple"

Night holds a scarlet moon.
I sneak out with the Evening Rain
Lilies* while the garden sleeps. I smuggle

the bumblebees' ears out with me
so we can hear the moon's wood-block voice.
The burden of my aloneness turns

my face butter-white.* *Sweetness will come,*
he says. *Your husband must pass through*
Europe's edges and Antarctica's troubles first.

Then, like a falling leaf, he will come to you.
He'll groan to tell you about several gaps
in his history, and his consequent thirst

for yours will follow. All the petals
you've gathered for him will be a welcome gift.
You won't always be a lonely sunflower.

---

*Evening Rain Lilies — flowers that bloom in the evening.
*Sunflower seeds turn white when they are not yet fully grown.[3]

Who Has my Husband
with select words from Li-Young Lee's "Evening Hieroglyph"

Who has you, I wonder? Who hears the wind go by
your ears since that always makes a sound? She will
find herself left behind in time. Her own true version
of your time together is a seed falling beneath her
to die and be born a dream of mine, the one dream
every cell of me has dreamed since infancy. Who has
twice served your hands to herself in a golden dish?
Who is double the trouble I will ever be? Who splits
her voice, asking more of you? While you sit on
the bed, who tugs at your feet? Who chirps, "Take me
home!" "Keep me!" Who will send you away with
a forever stamp straight to my yellow mailbox?

To the Husband I Haven't Found
with select words from Li-Young Lee's "Evening Hieroglyph"

keep changing places
in an empty tree

with the eastern screech-owl*
sip some tea   let me wilt

make no haste   be ever so still
face just one direction

flit from step to step
pretend not to notice me

looking up at you
from the dew-laden grass

---

*Eastern screech owls camouflage better than most other birds due to mottled markings that break up their silhouettes.[2]

How to Love Me

>with select words from Li-Young Lee's "Seven Marys,"
"Descended From Dreamers," "Parable of the Jar,"
"Little Ache," "Cuckoo Flower on the Witness
Stand," "After the Pyre," "The Sea With Fish,"
"Changing Places in the Fire," "God Seeks a
Destiny," and "Secret Life"

1. Find yourself.
2. Acknowledge your stars inside and out.
3. Don't be too much of a mystery.
4. Keep yourself safe and alive. Become invisible to near-death experiences.
5. Zero your lies on the scale before you come inside.
6. Decide the fate of us early.
7. Don't be late.
8. Press our adventures into the pages of your skin.
9. Answer my many questions, even if you don't know how.
10. Seek asylum from your illegible past, please.
11. Forget playing a Fine,-I'm-Just-Fine character, and show me your box of glass tears.
12. Have seven ancient colors. Tell me how "My father never…," and "My mother would always… ." Uncover your hidden strata*.
13. Allow yourself to pass mindfully through the fire of Trauma without running. Melt; save me from your explosion.
14. Know that screaming men will be caught in my pyre's updraft.
15. Find the words. I'll sit wherever you are; I'll wait with no grudge until you do.
16. Elect someone who cares that the grain is happy and the

*Strata — layers of rock.

sheep stay laughing.

17. Let me trace the pleats and figures that multiply on the mirror of your tongue.
18. Look out the window, but look at me too.
19. Learn the Sabbath is my favorite son, cherished and beloved. Make it yours too.
20. Ask about my origin.
21. Tell the oldest stories your grandfather told you, back from when he traversed the seven seas.
22. Help me pick out a triple oven.*
23. Measure out the right kitchen for my delight.
24. Dismantle our washer; I'm sorry I broke it with our synthetic-down comforter, but it's your fault for squeezing me like an orange.
25. Ask me kindly to fetch the crying baby inside our home. Gentleness must be your first language.
26. Don't fall asleep while our oldest child counts to nine hundred.
27. Climb into an apple tree with our daughter, and show her the parts of its fruits.
28. Photograph our children in their mother's garden, so we may have their pearl faces to look back on.
29. Turn any child from burning leaves to loving their colors.
30. Hand me a thrill when you smell the bread that rises in our kitchen.
31. Grow old at the dining room table with me so we may always have something shared and sacred.
32. Decades from now, continue forward. Don't throw me out with the bathwater.
33. Remember the ocean, shadows of windblown leaves, and

---

*Triple oven — an oven that allows a person to bake three items at once in separate compartments with individual temperatures.

the branches on the curtains of our honeymoon suite.
34. Help me pull the sheets tight on our bed each sunrise.
35. Piece our front-yard tree back together, or at least cut out the piece with our initials on it, so we can count its rings when we are equally as lined and brown.
36. Witness what keeps vanishing between us. Let's discuss it so it doesn't make us disappear too.
37. Pause if you don't know what I said, just as you would in a pine forest to hear a deer's apprehensive footsteps.
38. Sing. Laugh. Rest.
39. Breathe, cry, stare — postpone all morning bells if that's what you need.
40. Face each moving train with me and not alone.
41. Help me shift the panels on your Japanese-puzzle-box-mind — show me its infinite moving parts.
42. Allow me to sing you to sleep while I wrap a whole flower around your deepest wound.
43. Know that, no matter how high or low you go, I will walk, swim, crawl, climb, even grow wings if I have to, to sit with you and your storm cloud.
44. Wear skin that matches the red rocks on my favorite mountain and smells like the freshwater that crashes through its springs.
45. Watch old American TV.
63. Begin a new century when you meet me. Tell me that "all those years," you were looking for me with your telescope.
46. Open the pocket dictionary full of words in another language when I ask how to say *kiss me* in French.
47. Walk behind me unless you're holding my hand and leading me through a crowd.
48. Think of a needle and thread, or a living cloth, or scissors

trimming lament. Have a mind that imagines worlds.
49. Finely weave a net of rain on the imaginary surface of a pond, and ask me if I like it.
50. Speak to me in thoughts, dreams, and voice notes.
51. Divide every word between us, between what was heard and what was meant.
52. Ponder — is looking back a waste of time?
53. Believe me when I say I'm sorry, and let that be the end.
54. Be my faithful playmate.
55. Build a white fence between the women always looking at you and the woman always there.
56. Take me between earth and sky, to waterfalls, to heights that threaten my balance, but hold my hand all the way.
57. Dress my cheek in kisses by day; repeat the contours of my body by night.
58. That sparrow on the iron railing — do not let our child spear it.
59. Look at ears of wheat and grazing cows with me.
60. Keep the bees in their hive unless they come through my door.
61. Tell me the shape of the clouds above us now.
62. Hold any rat with a gentle clutch, and know that it's sorry for getting lost in our attic. Let it see the Pinedrops* again.
63. Lift flowers from the mountain for me, then let me thread them into a bursting table ornament.
64. Wait for me if your steps are bigger.
65. Change if you want, but try to hold onto the same man I fell in love with.
66. Look familiar when you come home each day unless it's Halloween.

*Pinedrop — a wildflower native to Colorado.

67. Tell me whether you like my hair down or tied up.
68. Love the dawn as much as I do, so we can watch the pink yawn of the sun as it awakens the candy-cane hills.
69. Sign the July sky with smoke, and give me your extra sparkler.
70. Show me the people that light up your face with bright blushes. But, notice when my hands tremble because their music is too loud, and rescue me.
71. Tell by my frown that I'm down in a double-cream-hurt-storm, and jump into it with me.
72. Revere how deserted I have been before you.
73. Believe the falling rocks that broke parts of me away.
74. Remember why I'm afraid of the ethereal dark — don't turn the lights off.
75. Arrive all night if I need you, and know I'll do the same.
76. Rock me in and out of moonlight.
77. Kiss my nose.
78. Set me on your lap, and move your fingers from rib to rib.
79. Change places with ice if I'm freezing. Cover me like a blanket.
80. Lift my heart out of black honey with a hot pan and a paper plate.
81. Tell God's seeing hand to send wind to untangle me from the branches of life if I'm caught in them.
82. Sound out encrypted sentences from my mind, and set them in my hand.
83. Be quick to remind me that earth's shadow will erase today.
84. Brush my cheeks with morning hues, and dry them lightly when tears spill from my weary eyelids.
85. Follow the lines of my hair with your fingers, like

they're Dutch tulip fields.
86. Shut the room's curtains if pain decides to play hide and seek in different corners of my brain.
87. Let me be alone sometimes, but not for too long.
88. Love me, even as I write your name thirty-one ways in my little notebook (and only sometimes crumple the paper).
89. Let my italic script fascinate you, and consent to our secret life being delineated in my inevitable publications.
90. Even if you think you can't, write me a poem.
91. Die with me instead of first.
92. Carry me back to our house if I swallow more than enough whiskey.
93. Every morning, tuck a promise into my pajamas and under my pillow.
94. Flea with me to an archipelago when it rains too hard for us to stay home, but tell your mother where we're going.
95. Be the eye, the heart, the dove that watches under and over me.

Winter Must Make a Good Wife
with select words from Li-Young Lee's "The Lives of a Voice: 4. My Joy"

Winter must make a good wife.
Wearing dawn as a gown, she steps

out of her blizzard bath, sun-kissed and ready
to be scooped. You can gaze at her

through any window — she makes herself ready
for your enjoyment. While you work, she sweeps

concrete floors with her wind-broom
and prepares a frozen killing.

Just before lulling you into an alpine sleep,
she showers you in a blinding love

that drags down the indigo curtains of moonrise.
Overnight, she washes and fluffs

your vanilla-cream bedspread and lays it out,
crisp, on the morning lawn.

Her smooth, cold hands brush you into waking —
she ensures your lips turn red as winter berries

before covering you in dutch-white linen,
creased under her slick iron.

SLATS

with select words from Li-Young Lee's "Virtues of a Boring Husband"

me / a house by the sea
whose roof builds itself /

every roof has hands
that clap when a gust blows /

the many hands of lovers /
lovers amount atop me /

every slat just like its neighbor /
my body shakes /

i am both sure and not sure /
and so emerges a ripple

on my ceiling /
quiet as a crow's footsteps /

in a garden /
i wonder what "right here" means

when people say they are /
how long will they stay   sleep

care   for my body / my arms
find their place in the fetal position /

along with the rest of me /

i calm myself from the thought

that a pair of hands will lie /
down beside me every hundred days /

only to toss and turn / the door knob /
the next evening /

feels exhausting /
what is a good night's sleep /

where is the magic i deserve /
is there room for a new slat /

To my Sister
with select words from Li-Young Lee's "First World"

When we were young, we could leap
into every season, could sink into dreams
and nights beyond the known stars. Then,
when the night was all tucked into bed,
we would close our eyes and empty the basket
of our minds to climb a jeweled staircase.
You and I would lay near the other, kept in
the bigger hands of God. Now, days are just
white notes in our orbit's greater song.
The days disappear like cards in envelopes.
Where is noon, or midnight, or the bridges
toward the future we wove out of wonder?
Did we climb those too?

Little Genevieve Understands Evil
*with select words from Li-Young Lee's "The Lives of a Voice: 2.
A Voice's Gaze"*

"Is it true that someday my rocking horse will splinter me,
my red wagon trip me, my sailboat drown?"

"Is it true that my orchard will be burdened
by the very icy crystals that cast cold rainbows

around my room at Christmastime?
Do you mean to say I can't fly

with a giant umbrella or step through time
like a windblown door? Is it true

that a starling's wings can be cut, that feelings
are bound by how loud we're willing to sing them,

that closed ears make a house grow feet,
and fire thrives among houses that walk barefoot?"

"Do you mean to say my body's curve
will be used against me?"

III. Think Tank

*"I know I was dreaming of knives and curtains
and stars and antlers and bees."*
— Julie Carr

Fever, Dream
with select words from Julie Carr's "✷," pages 24-27

Plum and buttered crackers
feed my stomach's flame.
Milk and sugar build
a ladder in my throat.

A fever lays on me,
a diaphanous* gown
that shivers my tender shoulders.
White-washed, I turn

my eyes to face the window.
I wear "part of a shirt,"
as an old woman called it.
I arch my mango feet,

pull on my peeled lip,
and hand the fan my ticket
to its cool-air parade
down my beaded forehead.

Lost in my sickness,
I heap napkins on my head
to gather the beads. Napkins
inflate into sugar cubes

that I climb to reach Saturn.
I put his rings on my finger
and scoop up some dust,
packing it like a snowball.

*Diaphanous — light / delicate / translucent.

I reach for a boiling star
and plant it in
his mustard mouth
to make him glow.

Out bursts a berry tree!
I crack open a plum,
and bluebirds plume out
from its pit. Wet plums

are cold and sweet,
their slight tang like a blade
on my tongue. Thirst.
I climb just far enough

down the sugar cube tower
to make Saturn as big as
a drinking glass. I sip
from his outer rim

until I can't anymore.
I set the striped glass
down on a cloud,
and it floats away.

"Leave Liquids Here" — TSA

with select words from Julie Carr's "★," pages 28-33

Boarding, a young woman drags through the aisle as though in mud. Thirst finds its way to her throat's roots, buried in her neck. Drought travels to her cheeks and tongue, soaking up what dampness remains. Thirst — what spawned as a gulch has become a ravine. The carousel of Wanting turns forever, her horse bound to its post with each pass. Even the horse's lips split open like cracked earth. Apples, apricots, milk, cream — nothing is as kind as water in a dry moment. Willpower, patience, and peace escape into the cabin floor. She imagines a library where every book opens to a water form: -droplet, -glass, -fall, -tower. By owl-light, she writes of a freshwater paradise, even as the thought of it strengthens her thirst. The sea, once a dream, becomes a repulsive notion with its salt upon salt. Its hypothesized granules pierce her imagination with their deceptive shine — a reminder of her pink, deprived, esophageal cells.

Attempting distraction, she concentrates on a screen in another aisle, senses the earth's spin, feels her aching foot, ponders the meaning of "relief," curses the cruel kiss of saliva — *my God*, she moans, sure that His back is turned to her.

Sudden wheels rumble over the dotted carpet — the beverage cart. Water — the deep ambition of her tongue. Her shaky hands receive a small, cold cup. Thirst is forgotten as water sinks into her lips, like snowmelt rushing into canyon cracks. Her stomach's floor — a thunderstorm of pleasure and contentment. A passenger's plump orange wedge no longer sparks exasperation. For a brief moment, misery is dead.

A Piece of Life
with select words from Julie Carr's "★," pages 12-17

All the way down the sun-studded avenue, I tell Grandfather's rosy, speckled face about Heaven. "You'll rise out of your feet like a lemon tree flowers: almost flowing, studied by God. It will be a new kind of living, an excellent condition. I've heard the mind suspends above the floor, that wheat fields and branches open wide. You'll enter another room. You'll have a melting body in timeless skin."

★

He lays still in his red, plaid shirt, my mother kissing his bright, sugar-coated cheek. I wonder if he knows I'm twenty-five now. My mother memorizes his bedside before leaving.

★

Empty, granite countertops balance the event of his death. To remind us of his euphonic★ chuckle and folk form,★ Bosc pears are displayed — his favorite fruit to eat with a Raisin-Bran muffin. For less than a day, it was normal that he'd died. Not hours later, his absence puzzles even the warm, cinnamon walls, and we are left asking, "What holiday is this?"

★

Outside, there's a blurry sun and fat tree limbs, pulpy and moist. Neighbors hatch from their houses to bring condolences. *There is no escaping me*, the tawny walls whisper. Hoarfrost on the windows reminds me that winter approaches with slight, crackling footsteps. Cold, gray stones mirror my skin tone. I'm without expression, blank as a yet-lit candle.

★Euphonic — pleasing to the ear / harmonious.
★Folk form — ordinary people who live a simple life.
★Hoarfrost — a grayish-white crystalline deposit of frozen water vapor formed in clear, still weather on vegetation, fences, windows, etc.

Funeral Ceremony as Parade
with select words from Julie Carr's "★," pages 21-22

In the blinding entourage
of violin strings, plucked and sharp,

I wave to the petals — fresh like butter —
to the done-up pears, to the coffee. I wave

to the light in someone else's velvet curtains
and wash clean my mother's footsteps

if she's not already done so with her tears.
Throw your condolences, your glass dishes,

your sustenance to me and her
as we ride by in dark hues.

WHEN ANYONE DIES
with select words from Julie Carr's "," pages 1-3*

i am like a bird in an oil-stained sea,
stifled and drooping —

memories of the latest death hover
like clouds over my rainy afternoon.

i wear my future around my face
as a knotted onyx scarf.

i know each member of my bloodline
will grow wings to become a starling,

that each will leave me
walking the "noble walk" of mourning.

will the spill drag me down
into a watery grave?

brief moments of distraction are garnets,
combed and folded through coarse sand.

What's in a Day

>   *with select words from Julie Carr's "★," pages 4-5*

a kettle boils / geese hobble / a girl spins through a draft / my sweater threads a full sob to rust my long arms / my time's gone to sorrow / a cracked door fails to close in mid-air / the sparkle i've been told is stuck permanently in my eye is now a faded star / the horizon collapses at seven-forty / fog and fatigue run home / in my eyes : a white clock / patters through lamplight / playing games with Order / what's in a night / spinning toward a slushy dusk / minutes weaken / down the flowers go : flattened blossoms all tucked in their garden beds / ruddy* petals / chill and limp / lead to my very quiet disappearance / my face tosses its shadow to France / while the arms of my rocking chair take off with my tired mouth / i throw myself over the ledge of my midnight chair and stare into dead time / i hug the banister / stair-steps gloat over their collective endlessness /

★Ruddy — a rosy color.

LIFE

with select words from Julie Carr's "★," pages 41-44

What is the point of "being" if that's all you get to do?
Bag the sea; man the sands as they try to escape

on the wind's wings. Hand a volunteer the wet,
heavy trees from a hurricane. Wish them goodnight.

Lie flat in rippled days, and read. Have birds place
large platters on a table — Life is a party.

Log the impermeable oil that clips the contagion
of the ocean's hello. Come to the ground

since Life will bring you there eventually. Aim less —
you'll only get where it wants you to go.

ESCAPES

with select words from Julie Carr's "," pages 56-72*

mute snow's bright light / trains left stranded on their tracks / an out-of-business arrow where motivation used to direct me / my white face — a carcass of hunger / the sky shifting to heat / the back of a swing swaying in my mind / *chocolate and lips and pills* / lips on my lap call my existence to their calming touch / my inside: blank and torn, earth and ocean forced together / *time has an edge* / my hand on his skin: a rare source of escape / *today is a vapor* / *every day is a hangover* / birds of paradise in my backyard tree / departure this morning / me, barren as a mollusk / singing hymns in the pew / the arms of a highway carrying me home, away from the risk of downtown / this sewn book written on many chair backs / *gold is just value hopping from hands to hands* / tedium breezing by / *i don't want to cry over the dishes* / God painting the hills red-orange / my sulky run to burn calories so i can eat my feelings later / the overflow of fantasy for the glance of a man i like to look up at / my magenta mouth from which the charm is gone / a duck pond with the low roar of storm clouds, almost fully awake / the body of a bird expanding, black and white / little unknowable stars / the gleam of my multicolored rug / a daydream of lying under the snow, under fresh pavement / my many agile steps down and up the canyon stairs / stuffing my grief under summer's turning leaves / speaking to a dog / pastures behind me on an afternoon drive / grass / plants that expect me to live so they can / my teeth, clean-blond, straighter every week / nudity in the bathroom mirror to grasp what's left of my beauty, whatever grief scraps / *what can we do for twenty minutes to pass a bundle of grueling moments?* / an imagined crown to force myself to behave like the elevated woman i truly am

Drew

with select words from Julie Carr's "★," pages 24-27

Like the end of a dream, I am blank and wordless. My spirit reels on the edge of collapse. My eyes are drained of their pupils. My ghost sobs. Dusk covers the dawn.

Drew, my once-sister, sleeps in another city with my heirloom emerald hidden in her sleeve. Her cold kiss of betrayal stings fresh on my cheek. I wonder when she shut fast the drapes on her character and how I looked when the curtain's feet stifled my breath.

Even the wind looks the other way when she passes. I'm not sure if it's so he won't have to look at her or because he's turning the other cheek.

My room is weary from the burden of truth. A dark aura swallows up its clean air, and the sharp corners of its walls are stuffed with Drew's small responses to my interrogation. Some time ago, her spirit packed a bag and set off on its way. It must be wandering around the icy ridges of Antarctica. It must've mailed back what it could of the cold to hold its place in Drew's soul. Her lungs will go the way of a smoker from the flecks of little lies she breathes, each a demon.

The street is white and fat today. The garage where she drove off with loyalty as a shotgun passenger gapes in despair. My chalky hands feel the line where I used to wear my grandmother's ring. My stare burns holes in the Persian rug beneath me, burgundy and silent.

A New Distraction

with select words from Julie Carr's "★," pages 50-51

Who's breathing? I can't tell the carbon braid
apart from our twisted-together mouths.

You draw curves on my spine I didn't know
I had. You draw with a touch made

of soft light and what's left of summer.
Find me — weave your fingers around mine.

Pull them like the chain on an electric lamp.
Send your energy through my meridians.

Look down at me from the high hill
on which your eyes sit.

Bring me into your cinnamon cotton;
cover me with grace.

Command for my Past
with select words from Julie Carr's "★," pages 50-51

Lie down, I say to my past, *near*
the slick sea where I sold you
last December. Give up your mission,
dry up in the sun, let go of my mouth,
and quit hanging onto my moments
of pleasure. Crawl into a lampshade;
be the dust I sweep from my dresser-top.
Leave my high spirit alone. Forget
my longing at your home. Let
my body turn over and over
without your hands grasping me.

This is What I See
with select words from Julie Carr's "★," pages 52-55

this is the brisk draft that awakens
my feet on October's porch
some mornings

this is the shadow of the pine tree
that waves to me when i open
my front door

this is the way to the park
my view of a bird
of a dandelion

this is the flattening of lilacs
from the rain
on my favorite mountain

these are the petals in my dreams
shiny reflections on a train
that i saw in venice

this is the time   six-forty-seven
and the dark cloud
that floats on me many days

this is the ridge along the right side
of my head where a scar rows
her boat day and night

these are the dream-remnants
that i decipher when i wake
and the sugar-faces of my children

this is my body in a dress
my hair under a lamp
the infinite lines of my fingerprints

this is my side that slumps
when i get too content
with life

this is a mark from my fiancée
and my belly where he left
a flower

this is the best way to lie
a reminder of my brutal resistance
to the anxious-memory catalogue

this is why i no longer demand
anything but respect and why
you're the only one who will speak at times

this is my desire for you
that pours   absolutely unwriteable
this is what i see

Escapes II

with select words from Julie Carr's "✶," pages 74-78

All heavy cups serve either a glossy silence
or fruitless sleep. My thoughts

are split-open walnuts in night's eleventh hour.
In these blank minutes, I swim

willingly into the few, candied memories
when you blushed to be near me. Indigo

and field green blend into strings that tie us
together and blissfully unravel when we part.

There's no uncomfortable pull, not even a strain —
only infinite thread, only the lowest murmuring

of white moths that flitter, slow and calm,
in my stomach. I feel you walking near me

even while you travel another city. There
isn't anything empty or too full about us —

not yet. Simmering hours of my day
are swallowed in gentle laps by the soft mouth

of our anticipated adventures. If I knew
I'd see you tonight, I'd climb the day's dust

with ease. For, you're my only true escape
from the all-encompassing walls of Grief.

IF I COULD MAIL-ORDER HIM
with select words from Julie Carr's "★," pages 34-38

I'd overnight him. The postmen would all become pilots to get him delivered in time. He'd have to hang on to his cabin seat with a rope as he flew. Over the ocean, a silver, fuzzy reflection would hover. I bet this wouldn't be what he had in mind when he imagined meeting his soulmate. All the same, he'd fall in love with the hazy windowpanes that shipped him to me as he curved over the sphere of our shared planet. After his travel, his left side would be scuffed with dirt, all of him mulberry silk,★ some edges snagged, a few corners pushed in. His right leg would be unevenly splashed with dried rainwater. Over the radio, they'd announce him: *One whole person, airborne — a fast cloud in love curving over Earth.* He'd be dropped at my doorstep and knock on my door. He'd tell me of his perilous evening over the waters and of his thoughts when he was notified of his orders. Then, he would be mine.

★Mulberry silk — naturally pure, white silk made from the cocoons of Bombyx mori moth silkworms, which are fed only mulberry leaves.[4]

After I Lock the Front Door
with select words from Julie Carr's "," page 10*

outside the house   orange scattered butterflies

tight glinting brick   that drives forsythia*

full in the face   up from the tears

of good-morning dew   twin plum trees

snowbound   wet   sprinkle my organdy*

dress   with their day shadows

*Forsythia — an ornamental Eurasian shrub that grows in temperate climates (such as Colorsdo) whose yellow flowers appear in early spring.
*Organdy — the sheerest cotton fabric in existence that is often used to make women's formal dresses.

IV. NO MATTER THE WRECKAGE

"Clouds unravel into spider webs."
— *Sarah Kay*

Night Walking

> *with select words from Sarah Kay's "Subway"*

come with me, lover.
slip between doors;

hop on top of a coming train —
hurry here.

come at night or
in rain; peer

through the strips
of dark blue evening.

let's splatter paint &
find brick walls to lean against.

hold my dress —
don't let me fall.

Numb Days

with select words from Sarah Kay's "Evaporate"

today i arrived so far away unfolded now i sit looking at my face in a mirror put on a dress i practice cracking my voice like a fresh egg in the morning i sound sick gray parts of me evaporate like nighttime dew before dawn

Broken Umbrellas
with select words from Sarah Kay's "Love Poem #137"

i wake up heavy & beat
i know you will leave me
the door is the difference between
me & someone sweeter than you
over the window sill
i look for you
i count my broken umbrellas
my many loveless lovers
one-hundred-thirty-seven
i fall asleep
i wake up heavy & beat

The Rush to the Bicycle
with select words from Sarah Kay's "The Toothbrush to the Bicycle Tire"

He's hot air I'm always chasing,
always watching disappear.

He tells me I'm mean
then drags me through the mud.

I dream he'll spin me around,
but I wake up dizzy.

His brown-sugar half-smile
pulls my porcelain ship along.

For the last time, we roll on into morning.
Now, he is lonely, and I'm on a bicycle.

Under Winter

with select words from Sarah Kay's "Bricklayer"

snow sits on brick layers,
on the cold edges of everything.
cold gloves hold warm hands.
worn hands litter the roadside.

somewhere very still and dark, there's
a wall built by a bricklayer — a wall
forged to keep cold in and warmth out.

but the bricklayer's back groans
from stacking. he bends down
for a brick; his flannel does not —
it rips. his fingers ache and chafe.

his cold-loving wall drops him,
frozen to death, in the snow.
cold gloves litter the roadside
near an unfinished wall.

i thought there would be a chance
of april flowers, but not this year.
the snow persists.

If I were a Book
with select words from Sarah Kay's "The First Poem in the Imaginary Book"

If I were a book, I would start by finding my name,
my body, my mother. I would tend to the evidence
of myself.

I'd locate a note that says for what purpose I was bound.
I might wonder if these found fingerprints
are your footsteps on my pages, my thoughts, my spirit.

I'd crack my spine and place myself
under a stack of papers to prevent someone
unworthy from reading me.

Alden's French Tulips
with select words from Sarah Kay's "Poppy"

I hold Alden's dress, the color of marmalade,
in my fingers. I read her hair like mist reads Avignon* fields.

I envision holding her like a clear glass vase
as she places her cool petals on my shoulder.

I wish for her to dip her garden in my sunbeams,
to drag her Dutch rows along my freckled skin.

She turns to water her French tulips,
And her yellow hair gathers to one side as she tips over.

Bend back and forth — I am the wind.
Let your water overflow into mine, I think.

Slip the moon's nightgown over your shoulders.
Sing and turn while the frostbite rises.

*Avignon — where French tulips are grown.

THE ANNIVERSARY OF HER ESCAPE
with select words from Sarah Kay's "Slivers"

Sweeping water returns you, limp. My dearest friend, you are a sliver of yourself. Look out from under the seagulls. See those beach umbrellas from our wooden pier? Walk with me through their banded colors. Take in the sand hills. Feel the hurt inside instead of twenty years later, but memorize and rehearse the truth of your story. Remove your feet from the ever-rising sand. Climb out from the whale that's swallowed you. See yourself and your symmetry in the shining mirror of the water.

As a Child

>   *with select words from Sarah Kay's "Mrs. Ribiero"*

I am a swish of silk outside my mother. My rib cage is the size of a nightlight. I grab a fist full of her hair and lift it to see how she floats.

I see hanging plants with stars on them. I throw a gentle knock at her ribs. I need to inspect that yellow star. She tells me the star is a succulent bloom, and she points to its petals.

The world uses every color to draw itself in my tetrachromatic* eyes. On a walk, brightly-pigmented caterpillars are almost as tall as me. *Please! Let me be one*, my head says, and my ribs reply, *We are many, stacked*.

Socks. Blocks. Toes. Look how much I know. My mother brings two rabbits and me into a fenced hexagon. We poke our noses through the fence's diamond-shaped holes. I bring one rabbit close to me — my ribs feel two warm hearts.

Suddenly — a high-pitched, repeating squeak. I study the sound with my ears. Large, dripping boots make their way to my palms. They feel cold and wet in my fingers. I wonder what they taste like and coax them into my mouth. Carpet threads brush my belly. I inspect their prickling texture.

My mother's gentle hands hold a Golden Book. Her voice meanders along the word path of each vivid page like dandelion seeds in a breeze.

*Tetrachromacy — possessing four cones in the eye instead of the usual three, allowing a person to experience a wider range of color than the average individual.

My Mother

with select words from Sarah Kay's "The Ladder"

my mother is the universe
she tells me to put stones underneath my home
"stones are sweet dreams"   she tells me
"each one is a spoonful of honey"
my mother bakes back and forth
across a bag of lemons   she giggles
she makes tea   she knows how i breathe
my mother is a warm laugh

The Mind-Path of a Child
with select words from Sarah Kay's "The Oak Tree Speaks"

I put my feet on the morning carpet. I listen. I ask my hand which way I should go and point.

Today, I remember which colored pencils I need to draw a starfish but not how to tie a ponytail.

Outside, boys wave at me across the lane. I whisper a great, big number to them. They try to count to it. We are sure about our answers. We hold hands.

Hands feel mountains and book pages and other hands. Palms clench paper or pound against dough for the oven. Fists can grip a violin or a zipper. They flatten together to form a prayer.

At lunchtime: look at my hands! They're yellow with mustard. I shake my head at them; I know it isn't right. A napkin drinks the yellow out of my palm.

The Potential Energy of a Child
with select words from Sarah Kay's "Brother"

A brown-haired girl wears a hibiscus-patterned sweatshirt. She also wears my shadow.

I understand more than you believe, she seems to say.

I sew a fork into her place-setting tablecloth while she traces a figure-eight with a wooden stick, mumbling to herself and nodding her head. Her voice heightens: "It is the 19th day of June. S is the 19th letter of the alphabet. G is the 7th letter, and my name begins with G."

She sorts a geographic puzzle on a floor mat, placing each continent in its position. She teaches herself where they go by feeling their edges.

With colored pencils, she draws the turning autumn leaves. She notes that "a narwhal's horn points straight up," and "carousel ponies actually keep people standing on their toes."

She walks in every direction, whether or not her compass points north, just to see what's around.

She notices the moment a train comes to a stop and how satellites dip in and out of the night sky.

She knows how to find thunder. She giggles at her own hiccup.

Ride Home From The Blue Fish Restaurant, 2007
with select words from Sarah Kay's "New York, June 2009"

Sirens hollow out dusk raindrops.

A woman's round waist almost rolls down her hourglass figure.

A wheelchair on the curb is lifted into a truck bed.

A houseless dog's leather paws slump like a grandfather.

A missing girl is posted on three telephone poles.

The wrinkles in Dad's "Nice Shirt" collect yellow lights.

A frail praying mantis grips the rubber around the car window.

Traffic folds my ears over. One horn makes me breathe in for a count of four.

A Daydream

with select words from Sarah Kay's "Fish"

day sinks, pink and orange, into a crystal afternoon.

under the shade of a white umbrella, my toes toss sand into the breeze.

i count twenty-two motions of a sandpiper's beak probing the shore's shiny gloss.

sand crabs seep like ink around my ankles. i walk.

off the jetty, i scrutinize a rogue tentacle's pattern, long like a railroad, as it thwalms down the back of my hand.

purple circles are caught in my fingers until the small octopus slips between two rocks.

her slurping echoes out like ripples as the seawater whips itself into cotton candy.

Autobiography of a House
with select words from Sarah Kay's "Montauk"

I am seven years old. Drifting forsythia blooms pack themselves into yellow, spotted bunches, resting in my porch puddles on rainy afternoons. An apricot tree beside me entices my hardware to loosen, putter, and giggle when she drops her fruit in my lap. I brave the full-length rush of this season's waterstorms, but eventually, I bend. I am small and butterscotch and glowing as you glide past me, toss your hair, and wish on stars.

5G

with select words from Sarah Kay's "My Parents on Their Way Home From a Wedding"

all i can see is a 5G tower
all i can hear are dings from notifications

i think we got lost
sometime after street corners were invented

driving on highways   laughing on speakerphone
inhaling dusty air
posting other people's wedding ceremonies just to get
affirmation

why isn't there a time for
streaked sunlight
guitar harmonies
wind
a few seconds

you should hear the symphony inside the cabin
when the plane lands

Train From Rome to Florence
with select words from Sarah Kay's "The Oak Tree Speaks"

Glass marbles roll down a single stair and hop into hands,
growing small.
A boy runs in reverse.
Rooftops pile up on each other.
A middle-aged tree folds over into the ground.
I press a dark, metal frame with my arm, cold
from the pressurized cabin.
Ribbons of corn ears wave to adjacent winds
as the train slows.
In a coffee cup, a smeared oak tree covers a smeared man
breathing. He stops.

>Escape growing up — age pays a price.
>A wheel is just two smiles stacked.
>When a tree dies, count the rings —
>notify the other trees.
>Watch your heart grow.
>Take in the cornfields and sky.
>Go straight for any apple pie.
>Notice if something's missing,
>anytime, anywhere.

V. THEN WINTER & THE TULIP-FLAME

> "To love her is to accept she will
> never turn around."
> — Chloe Honum

September 7th

> *with select words from Chloe Honum's "April in the Berkshires"*

Beside me,
rain climbs
the windows.

Behind my stack
of pillows, my wardrobe
embraces me.

Beneath my quilt,
I roll over and wrap
my arms around themselves.

Cold Front

> *with select words from Chloe Honum's "First Day of Partial Hospitalization"*

in a common parking lot
snow is born
trucks swallow far away hills
as a brief winter blows in

Surroundings

with select words from Chloe Honum's "Offerings"

The sky lies in the laps of blue spruce trees.
Ripples carry sunlight to rest underwater.
Rushing up like flames: the cold song of Wind.
Rain droplets spin webs in my hair.
A field of fireweed* holds a child playing in the sun.

---

*Fireweed — Rocky Mountain wildflower named for its tendency to colonize areas impacted by wildfires.

Play

> *with select words from Chloe Honum's "Blossoms in the Psychiatric Ward"*

"Play" is an idea first,
a verb, second. Play folds
and re-folds like a handkerchief.

His face hides in heavy,
browning blossoms,
disorganized.

Beyond the window, he bobbles
in the rain, twinkling
and tear-streaked.

Under a living-room carpet's fringe,
Play tosses and turns. Whether he's
coming or going, no child can say.

Timeline of a Tuesday From a Child's Perspective

with select words from Chloe Honum's "Lunch Break at the Psychiatric Ward"

Morning
Awake in a yellow house
Climb down narrow stairs
Watch cartoons
Tap the glass of the fish tank
Feel the tickle of a silk carpet's blue bristles

Afternoon
Gaze outside — gray
Admire the birds in the trees' hair
Mom pours me a cup of tea
A butterscotch fluff rolls over on my toes
Many silver hours tick by on the grandfather clock

Evening
Eat a dinner roll
God paints the sky pink
Dad wraps me in a cotton blanket
The attic creeks
I drift to sleep

9TH STREET

> *with select words from Chloe Honum's "On the Stairs Outside the Psychiatric Ward"*

A twisted body
of smoke deforms
the almost-dark.

All around, gold
and crimson leaves
latch onto the cold.

A string of birds
and sky resolves into
a web of clouds.

Daylight Savings

> *with select words from Chloe Honum's "The Angel"*

Hours before Autumn's tumble through time, my toes
trace midnight alleys and make curbs into balance beams.

One alley's insomniac stream trickles by me in a crystal braid.

I imagine I have cotton balls for feet and hop back and forth
over the water.

Suddenly, my steps slip on a shining shadow: a knee-length
garden gown.

Its julep* middle clings to the curb above the gutter, bright
from the faint glow of a streetlight.

Seafoam silk ruffles in the river, whose blotchy grip persists
around her edges.

A mottled language bubbles up from the storm drain — it
gulps down memories of her swept-along hem.

The sapphire night pushes on as Autumn inches toward
reversal.

After a Poetry Reading
with select words from Chloe Honum's "The Ward Above"

I slide my hand through the night,

feeling for a lamp chain. Beside my door,

sunflowers welcome me home. After

the doorway, my wooden shelves float

past me. I place a half-read collection

on the entryway shelf and slide my hand

through the night, feeling for a lamp chain.

For the Holidays
with select words from Chloe Honum's "Note Home"

to see my mother
i must pack a dog and
my heart in a suitcase

years hum as this ritual repeats
as i name each object
that travels with me

*velvet dress   crystal earrings   chamomile
sheeps' wool   sparkling socks   sunflower
seeds   cherry juice   tin-can telephone*[10]

A String of Days That Ends with Light
with select words from Chloe Honum's "Stay Beside Me"

Three days rise and fall,
silent and afraid of the sun.

A wind chime jingles quietly
under a blanket of clouds.

Shade hovers over a lost ball
while rain plays on a shared mailbox.

Arriving Home

> *with select words from Chloe Honum's "Late Afternoon in the Psychiatric Ward"*

a horsefly with wet wings
twirls in between drops of rain
on my porch pavement.

a small waterfall spilling over
my roof resembles words
scribbled on top of each other
and dumped over a hillside.

dancing onyx shadows kiss my
woven welcome mat, signaling
my eyes to the moth-party
inside my porch lamp.

why aren't shadows sturdier
than a cardboard fort? why do
words push people underwater?
why can't the dead kiss my
cheek again?

At the Bus Stop

with select words from Chloe Honum's "We're Supposed to Get Snow Tonight"

A fog lays down
over my town.
The wind
grows colder.
Crows arc
overhead.
On the sidewalk,
a toad sits, paused
near a paper cup
and a Gladiola.
I wrap my hands
around the brown,
heaving lump.
My boots step
across a soft hill,
and I paint
a patch of grass
bronze
with my shadow.
I open
my toad-filled palms
into the field.
His spots twinkle
like pebbles in a stream.

Found Item I Will Use for a Stereognostic* Mystery Bag

with select words from Chloe Honum's "Group Therapy"

A black velvet sack waits beyond the trees,
hidden but in-focus.

The creek splashes, throwing silver dots
on the propped pouch.

Sunshine highlights the dropped plums
around it —

pearls scattered on a shoreline.
I want to know: who's your mother?

Crimson leaves gather around it.
Now, I have something new to dust off.

---

*Stereognostic — a sense defined by the ability to identify an object without looking at it.

Exam Preparation

with select words from Chloe Honum's "The Master of Dreams"

My crackling notes ruffle in the jet stream
while a traveling maple leaf catches on my
drawing of a boat.

The habit of my mid-day apple whisks
away its appeal, my desire silent.

Close behind me, my scarf, whose fabric
flaps like a hibiscus in an ocean gust,
doesn't answer when I call it.

NIGHT RUN IN MARKET SQUARE
with select words from Chloe Honum's "Early Winter in the Psychiatric Ward"

Jumping to enter the present,
I observe a woman
night-dancing
under a starlit sky.

A light mist comes in,
falling in feathery waves.
Geese. Darkness. Rags
in the charcoal road.

Old, heavy stories drag
along the starless paths
of my wild mind.

On my Way to the Bookstore

with select words from Chloe Honum's "Before Group Meditation"

On a borrowed bicycle, I pedal
through brisk November air.

Around a stone corner,
a little basketful of ordinary rocks
topples over jutting juniper roots.

Following close behind it
is a curious, purple dress.

"Genevieve, Genevieve!"
A boysenberry sweater with
a fizzling, moon-colored braid

motions the purple dress
toward her through the wind.

Photograph of my Mother's Morning Walk (1998)

with select words from Chloe Honum's "Rest"

Morning's first tide of light sweats. Impossible,
cloudless raindrops decorate the grass.

She wears a sweater woven of saffron threads,
and a string of black pearls garnishes her neck
like birds on a wire.

Freshly-cut newspapers lay like bouquets
on each neighborhood's doorstep.

Discarded magnolia petals absorb ink,
sleeping like dreams on a bed of letters.

LOVE AT FIRST SIGHT
with select words from Chloe Honum's "Phoebe"

I walk to the other side of the street,
passing a Water's Street Bank. I glance
through its glass. Tiny boots tumble
through a brass-framed door; marble
tiles complement the child's pink face.
Noon climbs through the glass building,
scattering white squares onto the walls.

Haven From Stalker / Journal From Hotel

with select words from Chloe Honum's "The Motel"

three brass numbers / under a night-lamp / inside a drop of rain / a series of doors / flat in my hands / night / thin curtains / silver clouds / one flight higher than the hatted bell-person that brought up my bag / i / blown inside-out like an umbrella / push my feet under cool white sheets / at last i sleep

as last i sleep / push my feet under cool white sheets / blown inside-out like an umbrella / i / one flight higher than the hatted bell-person that brought up my bag / silver clouds / thin curtains / night / flat in my hands / a series of doors / inside a drop of rain / under a night-lamp / three brass numbers

The In-Between Days

> *with select words from Chloe Honum's "My Great Aunt Billie at Ninety-Two"*

How often does he return to the days
after me in his wiser life? I wonder
what changed him in that time,
and what girl he walked into after me,
what tiny birds saw him kiss her
with charred lips. Does he come back
often to the days just before her
but after me? If so, how often does he?

Sunset

with select words from Chloe Honum's "At America's Best Value Inn in Crossett, Arkansas"

rabbitbrush* waves to my window
bending to the sunset-wind
clotted treetops sway in the evening
my beige fingerprints close the door
september fire twirls like butterflies
up the chimney   my feet linger   pale
the aluminum fence around the heat-giver
is a repurposed canoe

*Rabbitbrush — a colorful shrub native to Colorado.

Morning Dew

with select words from Chloe Honum's "Ballerina in Winter"

straight through the hills,
i carry birds like luggage
through a violet sky.

i change from wet concrete
to grande jetés. i go softly
around the neighborhood

like the reel on a cassette tape.
heavy chairs wait patiently
by the compost — i settle

on one with multicolored stripes.
weary from walking the avenues,
i lay down in a valley to sleep.

Gardening

with select words from Chloe Honum's "Hunt"

The grass rustles. A pair of houses

is pale gold in the drowsy morning.

Trumpet flowers climb out

of the light's loose skin. Fresh earth

is warm in my fingers.

Notes From a New State
with select words from Chloe Honum's "Spring II"

new to the state   frightened   jealous
alone at the end of a garden   stiff and still

i don't want to scare him away but i get darker
every day   slim and slimmer   without his call

on the lawn watching the sun set alone
its white knuckles before my eyes
are fading light — my intuition over time

i wish for a new day's yellow grip and wait
another whole night awake for him
to never call or show

sadly it's a beautiful afternoon
but i am stuck in an evening

The Illness of Beauty
with select words from Chloe Honum's "Snow White"

The illness of beauty is its power to lure you into it, almost drowning you in its wet, colored seasons. Its vast field is quicksand in a desert, and you are a lonely tree. A prince tells you he's coming to save you, to keep waiting, to be patient. Crows swoop and dive at your thinning hair strands, and over and over, the sun sets, a black fire behind you. Reeling becomes exhaustion. Stillness and imagined hope become a place to settle. Life moves backward. Like shadows in a cave, dreams grow larger. The moon cradles you since no one else will. Each night, you both thin as starlight weakens.

On the Anniversary of my Escape
with select words from Chloe Honum's "Leaving the Hospital"

Cloud shadows stream through grass and afterlight
in the first moment of winter.

On this anniversary of my escape, I turn
with a ruby face to confront my bitter past —
cocoa before processing.

I remember how we spoke.
I remember the mess he made of my heart.
I walked out amid his crushing words.

My heart sags, drained and angry but free.

I'm whole, and I don't have his glass fists
threading needles through my composure.

I'm lucky he won't come home again.

What If Everything Wasn't a Lie
with select words from Chloe Honum's "Hours"

what if everything wasn't a lie
what if he did what he said

i imagine

he returns after a year
a wheel of air turns slowly in my mouth
waiting to be released in a boat of laughter

my throat holds an eclipse of moths that jump
and cheer as i see him walking here

i stroll onto the porch thinking its a few steps closer to him
that i would see him sooner if i were that much nearer

we make our home upstairs above the trees
it is lovely to discard loneliness and curl into wanting arms

touching him is touching soft earlike folds
of mushrooms[5]

we do this for hours

About Silence

with select words from Chloe Honum's "Evening"

I want to tell someone about Silence —
about how, when a neighbor boy opens
his bedroom window toward me,
it bounces between us; how on
the porch in evening, its eyes will not
adjust; how it holds up a golden moon
in the wind and the leaves that all have
each other whisper in it at dark.

SHE WAS HAPPY
with select words from Chloe Honum's "Visiting Hours"

she's happy   she wants to live   suddenly
she gasps for frozen air   to calm an adrenaline leak*
in her system   she opens her window's latch   it sticks

her body: cold   her voice: a stone
she: a trembling ballerina   a white scarf
limp   on a metal frame

she was happy   she wanted to live
but her system: overwhelmed   her last breaths
wrung out her spirit and shut her mouth

---

*In select individuals, an overabundance of adrenaline causes sudden panic attacks; this reoccurrence is labeled as Panic Disorder.

LETTER TO GOD
with select words from Chloe Honum's "Ballerina at Dawn"

lift these passing rains   for a moment.

cover my pale veins   with a stretched cloud.

under the pelt,   see us both disappear

into the forest's widening mist.

To See You

with select words from Chloe Honum's "Nursing Home"

To meet you
To bring you lavender stems
To call your name
To fall flat
To laugh in sadness together
To clear your head
To say eight words in an hour
To find you in a chair or the garden
To help you look for a lost item or your mind
To say good morning
To see you
Would be nice

Tryst*

with select words from Chloe Honum's "Come Back"

Every hour closer to our tryst, my sanity
loosens. A snowy evergreen drips with worry
outside my bedroom window. Suspense
hides in pink threads on berries
from the backyard bushes. I can't see past
the flowing moon. Our future weaves
in and out of view. What if we meet, and the sky
drains of color? Will our day enter dusk?
What if fate drops a bloodstain on my ivory
dress, and my heart spirals, a red kite?

Between us, there's only a wish — the hope
of light. What if my desire gets lost,
like a dog's wet nose in the pleats of a skirt?
The drapes of our affair pull back and shut closed
with my undulating anxiety. The rain-sown ground
of a possible end threatens our white romance
before its dawn. If only I could climb
the fence to catch sight of our neighboring moments.
What's past the twilight of our future?
I shiver, waiting for reality to rush in like the cold.

*Tryst — a secret meeting.

The Encounter

with select words from Chloe Honum's "Fever"

I need to hold your next expression
with my eyes, in my hands.

Patience swallows me while I wait
to see how you take up space in a room.

Anticipation has grown into a whole storm
of orchestra tunes. I imagine making

out the beginning of your bright face
through a salty haze, my readiness

shape-shifting to fit herself
through the thin gap of the doorway

in which you stand. I imagine
lilac light falling over us like a veil.

Passing the Patisserie*

with select words from Chloe Honum's "Last of the Ballerina I Was"

My lips split. My eye-corners ripple. My cheeks
match the sunset. You and I walk through dusk
on square-rounded cobblestones. Our fingers slip
in and out of each other. Finally, I can put a face
to the man always in my imagination. Your short,
shining hair strands catch ascension in the wind.
I am sure of you, and you're sure of me. I hear
violin notes riding the breeze.

*Patisserie — a French bakery.

Holiday Drizzle
with select words from Chloe Honum's "June in Arkansas"

In a drizzle, I walk home toward night.
My heart turns as quickly as a moment
while I consider new romance. I shake
the peach stones* around my wrist.
Inside, on an olive couch, I read
a few silver words. I think of him.
Rain turns the slats on my roof
while remnants of apricot light pour
down the walls like wax. My chest is hot.
Do my ribs hold my heart down,
or will she leap through their bone-grate
into a man's ripe throat?

*Reference to the last poem in *Violet Afternoon*.

Depression Hour
with select words from Chloe Honum's "Dressing Room"

i forget what to do
if it's suddenly hard to breathe.
i am small and cold. where are you
to reassure me? i look for you
in our old conversations. i grow dim
as a chandelier with a few light bulbs out.
around the edge of my frilled uterus,
moths attach themselves to form
a rounded quilt. pairs of wings curl
like eyelashes while i stretch out
my compact abdomen. i wear a costume;
i unzip it each night before bed
or sometimes when i'm alone
in the mirror. my costume looks
like the surface of a pond,
my anxiety, fish beneath its glass.

The Cure

with select words from Chloe Honum's "Revenant"

all that it would take:
white flowers,
a clump of cold,
the sun,
a clean house,
a bowl of morning,
a spoonful of you.

In my Dream of Us
with select words from Chloe Honum's "December"

in my dream of us
at night   & sometimes
in the day   it snows
the white day welcomes us
& we sit behind the window
for a long time.

What We'll Share
with select words from Chloe Honum's "Leaving Town"

stars in blue winter,
dusk, shadows, hands,

a raw sound through leafless trees,
empty highways,

moving across a map,
a gentle focus,

two pretty voices — hopefully, three someday,
drifts of snow that hurry to melt away.

BRUSH

with select words from Chloe Honum's "Sixteen"

meet the darkness with your fingers
crawl to the tips of my toes
let your gaze glide over my whole person
like blades on fresh ice
but also study my eyes: fireflies

look at my intricate quilted pattern
pull my skin tight like a ribbon
but untie me like a bow
make my skincoat wet and shimmering
brush against me   make little mirrors

wake to me like i to the dew
fill my world with your small noise
soon   swishing hair will rest
light will cover us in spring
our shoulders deep in its waves

Let Yourself Be Loved
with select words from Chloe Honum's "To the Anorexic"

let your wrist be like a balloon
that's been floating for a few days.

feel the tug of surrender like poppies
that reach for the sky while sewn

to the ground. expect your shoulders
to be wrapped in joy, in my arms

around you. you are satin in my lap.
let morning fall on the other side

of this night. can you imagine
me sewing that hole in your sock

threading a snowflake
over the gap?

Airport Roses
with select words from Chloe Honum's "Crossing the Three-Rope Bridge"

My hands grasp a bundle in front of me.

Velvet's sharp colors rush past my focus

and into my arms. My world slips into

blurry swirls of red, and my cheeks turn

like pinwheels to match the ruby shades.

Endorphins sew tight ropes out of my back

muscles, forcing me upright like a nutcracker,

just in time for me to lower the roses and linger

on the edge of your familiar, softening kiss.

Love's Beginning*

with select words from Chloe Honum's "Bright Death"

My mind's changed — I don't want love to feel like tumbling through the air or down a hill.[11] I'd like this time to be different. I want both feet on the ground. I'd like to be so married to gravity that I'm laying in the grass with you next to me.

Let's make love from the tattered pieces of our past lives. I want patches to be sewn from the grass we lay in, so it's equal parts you and me. Let's make a new fabric of our own; let's make a quilt; let's make slow loops around each other. Let's make love as thick as a cloud so we can be close, so we can be warm in winter.

---

*In conversation with "Jack & Jill" from *The Moon Reaches For Me.*

What We Have

with select words from Chloe Honum's "Silence Is a Mother Tongue"

Gazes between us sparkle in the air.
Tomato sauce bubbles pop and kiss the pot,
thickening as my mind stirs.

In the kitchen, I am grateful for
our winter garden, for the days that turn
over like oars, for my heavy roses that sit,
crimson and wild in the window.

I rest like a fallen kite in the knowledge
that we have something like this,
our shimmering little corner of the world
that has a boiling pot and our favorite song.

Chapman Drive*

with select words from Chloe Honum's "Spring"

sunlight drops through cedar limbs

daisies bow in the grass

browning petals among the birds float

like little coins down the mountain

a wet winter coat thaws in a trench beside the trail

a boy kisses my cheek in the cold, clear air

i remember "all that falls is caught."[6]

*Chapman Drive is a trailhead in Boulder, Colorado.

Pond Lily

with select words from Chloe Honum's "Directing the Happy Times"

In nature's dim lights, you enter —
you've waited for this.

Your steps are precise, your hands
fully engaged, white, grabbing
my citrine skin like a vine.

You set me like a petal on your tweed couch.

Like a honeybee in a rainstorm,
longing knocks you down on top of me.

I turn over to bloom for you and float
on your weight like a pond lily.

You hum and blush, drawing me
like an illustration into a deeper hue.

Your fingers rush to get me out
of my headspace as though my mind
were a woman in wet clothes.

December 9th
with select words from Chloe Honum's "Dress Rehearsal"

Snow rests in low light.
The fire is a field
of ashes, climbing away
on smoke-air-balloons.
Shadows sleep and wake
on the left wall.
Something like a crow
seems molded
out of black —
its own ballet master
hopping by the studio
window. It plays
hide-and-seek
with the film of ice
that crawls across
each pane,
trimmed with silver.

Morceau de Temps*

with select words from Chloe Honum's "Danse des Petits Cygnes"

At Genevieve's wedding,
I sway in green velvet
with you. The leaves
become violins for her,
while the sound of her
white roses mirrors
us together. I yearn
for another song.

*Morceau de temps — French for "piece of time."

A Noticing
with select words from Chloe Honum's "Alone with Mother"

between us is a kind silence,
one like a sand dollar on the warm sea-floor:
a long ocean of beautiful moments.

can i bottle it? can i bottle the sea at dusk?

I Come Home To
with select words from Chloe Honum's "The Tulip-Flame"

one astounding hill
the midpoint of a wet field

rabbits' ears that flare out
and fray   dripping flowers

a watery cement path
at the end of a lane

a few crimson pages
dog-eared to make up my house

rolling brush holding the pages
together   windows

that highlight glinting
arrows of cold

Another Burning of Estes Park
with select words from Chloe Honum's "Ballerina, Released"

Smoke shakes the outlines of crackling morning frost. Fall turns from butterscotch trees to the flaming West. How can I sleep? A new book tells me, "*The moon is spinning in a sack of mist.*"[10] Over the grass, this couldn't be truer. Along fir boughs, a hummingbird hops and flitters. It no longer sings, but coughs. Dust stirs in the light like milk froth. Loose, tin, mail flags seem tangled in the wind. Their red arms hurry up and down as if to signal all night travelers East.

How This Book Was Made
with select words from Chloe Honum's "The Good Kind"

1. I found phrases:
~~it sounds~~
~~steamy grass~~
~~while making love~~
~~we don't hear it~~
~~the good kind~~
~~always there~~
~~our hands~~
~~your memories of me~~
~~i hope you don't~~
~~leap~~
~~ease off~~
~~begin~~
~~the summer rain~~
~~finally make it~~

2. I rearranged them:
summer rain begins and leaps in our hands
on steamy grass. while making love,
we don't hear it. i hope you don't ease off.
your memories of me, always there,
are the good kind. the rain sounds heavy
when we finally make it out.

ACKNOWLEDGMENTS

To my family — Thank you for unconditionally supporting my passion for book writing. Your reading of my work and your encouragement to keep writing lift me up.

To Catherine Stauber — Thank you for telling me that the color yellow is scientifically proven to make people happy and for giving me Olivia Gatwood's *Life of the Party*, which inspired this entire collection. Thank you also for affirming my talent, for your encouraging words, and for always getting a piece of cake with me to talk things over.

To Carlos Fernandes II — Thanks for putting up with me, allowing me to access your epic edits, and, most importantly, doing life with me.

To Chloe Honum, Li-Young Lee, Julie Carr, Olivia Gatwood, and Sarah Kay — Thank you for writing such inspirational words and providing me with the vocabulary to express new ideas.

To Jacob Shores-Argüello — Thank you for teaching me the tenets of poetry. Now, I can teach others how to get the most out of their writing.

REVIEWS

Leave a review of this collection on annafrazierpoetry.com in the "contact" section.

Reviews help the author's collection to be viewable by a wider audience, so others can share the experience that you have just had reading the collection.

Notes

1   Peter. "Georges Seurat: 1886 One Sunday After-noon in the Island of La Grande Jatte." 2021, Flickr, Web.

2   Keffer, Ken. "Birding Basics to Camouflaged Birds." Birds&Blooms, birdsandblooms.com. Accessed 10 December 2021.

3   "Why Are My Sunflower Seeds White: Sunflower Seeds and Its Harvesting?." *Modern Gardening Tips*, moderngardeningtips.com. Accessed 28 April 2022.

4   Garis, Mary Grace. "What is Mulberry Silk? Meet the Luxe, Eco-Friendly Fabric That'll Do Your Hair and Skin Some Serious Good?" Well + Good, wellandgood.com. Accessed 17 Dec 2021.

5   Honum, Chloe. "Hours." *The Tulip-Flame*. Cleveland, Cleveland State University Poetry Center, 2014.

6   Honum, Chloe. "Ballerina, Released." *The Tulip-Flame*. Cleveland, Cleveland State University Poetry Center, 2014.

Books

1. Carr, Julie. *Think Tank*. New York, Solid Objects, 2015.
2. Gatwood, Olivia. *Life of the Party*. New York, Penguin Random House, 2019.
3. Honum, Chloe. *Then Winter*. Durham, Bull City Press, 2017.
4. Honum, Chloe. *The Tulip-Flame*. Cleveland, Cleveland State University Poetry Center, 2014.
5. Lee, Li-Young. *Behind My Eyes*. New York, W. W. Norton & Company, Inc., 2008.
6. Kay, Sarah. *No Matter the Wreckage*. Austin, Write Bloody Publishing, 2014.

Chapter Quotes

1. Gatwood, Olivia. "We All Got Burnt That Summer." *Life of the Party*. New York, Penguin Random House, 2019.
2. Lee, Li-Young. "Become Becoming." *Behind My Eyes*. New York, W. W. Norton & Company, Inc., 2008.
3. Carr, Julie. "★." *Think Tank*. New York, Solid Objects, 2015.
4. Kay, Sarah. "Forest Fires." *No Matter the Wreckage*. Austin, Write Bloody Publishing, 2014.
5. Honum, Chloe. "Seated Dancer in Profile." *Then Winter*. Durham, Bull City Press, 2017.

www.ingramcontent.com/pod-product-compliance
Lightning Source LLC
LaVergne TN
LVHW041757060526
838201LV00046B/1033